Series/Number 07-156

D0141510

MEDIATION ANALYSIS

Dawn Iacobucci
Owen Graduate School of Management, Vanderbilt University

Los Angeles • London • New Delhi • Singapore

Copyright © 2008 by SAGE Publications, Inc.

All rights reserved. No part of this book may be reproduced or utilized in any form or by any means, electronic or mechanical, including photocopying, recording, or by any information storage and retrieval system, without permission in writing from the publisher.

For information:

SAGE Publications, Inc.
2455 Teller Road
Thousand Oaks, California 91320
E-mail: order@sagepub.com

SAGE Publications India Pvt. Ltd.
B 1/I 1 Mohan Cooperative Industrial Area
Mathura Road, New Delhi 110 044
India

SAGE Publications Ltd.
1 Oliver's Yard
55 City Road
London EC1Y 1SP
United Kingdom

SAGE Publications Asia-Pacific Pte. Ltd.
33 Pekin Street #02-01
Far East Square
Singapore 048763

Printed in the United States of America

Library of Congress Cataloging-in-Publication Data

Iacobucci, Dawn.
  Mediation analysis / Dawn Iacobucci.
     p. cm. – (Quantitative applications in the social sciences; 156)
  Includes bibliographical references and index.
  ISBN 978-1-4129-2569-3 (pbk. : acid-free paper)
     1. Social sciences—Mathematical models. 2. Structural equation modeling.
  3. Regression analysis. I. Title.
  H61.25.I13 2008
  519.5'36--dc22

                          2007046632

This book is printed on acid-free paper.

08   09   10   11   12   10 9   8   7   6   5   4   3   2   1

Acquisitions Editors:	Vicki Knight and Sean Connelly
Editorial Assistant:	Lauren Habib
Production Editor:	Cassandra Margaret Seibel
Copy Editor:	QuADS Prepress (P) Ltd.
Typesetter:	QuADS Prepress (P) Ltd.
Proofreader:	Kevin Gleason
Indexer:	Joan Shapiro
Cover Designer:	Candice Harman
Marketing Manager:	Stephanie Adams

Quantitative Applications in the Social Sciences

A SAGE PUBLICATIONS SERIES

Quantitative Applications in the Social Sciences

A SAGE PUBLICATIONS SERIES

CONTENTS

LIST OF FIGURES AND TABLES

ABOUT THE AUTHOR

Dawn Iacobucci is Professor of Marketing at the Owen Graduate School of Management at Vanderbilt University. She teaches marketing models and multivariate statistics. Her research focuses on networks, customer satisfaction, and statistical methodology. She has published in a variety of journals in marketing and psychology, such as *Psychological Bulletin*, *Psychometrika*, *Journal of Marketing*, *Journal of Marketing Research*, and *Marketing Science*, edited the *Journal of Consumer Psychology* and *Journal of Consumer Research*, and is author of *Marketing Management* (2009) and coauthor of Gilbert Churchill's lead text on *Marketing Research* (2007).

SERIES EDITOR'S INTRODUCTION

Social science data analysts have long considered the mediation of intermediate variables of primary importance in understanding individuals' social, behavioral, and other kinds of outcomes. For example, in epidemiology and health studies, it has been typical to study the effect of socioeconomic status (SES), often represented by an individual's educational attainment, on health outcomes, be they objective or subjective. Similarly, decades of research in social demography have presented time and again the importance of examining education or other SES variables for their mediating effects on fertility. If we use X to represent a background variable or determinant, Y an outcome variable, and M an intermediate or mediating variable, then two types of research described above may be summarized by $X \rightarrow Y$ and $X \rightarrow M \rightarrow Y$. That is, there exist both the direct effect of the background variable on the outcome variable and the indirect effect mediated by the intermediate variable.

Indeed, this type of causal thinking may find examples in virtually every single social science that applies statistical methodology, and that is likely why my predecessor, former editor Michael Lewis-Beck, saw value in encouraging Dawn Iacobucci to submit a book prospectus in the first place. Her finished book should fit in the series nicely with many existing volumes, including No. 34 *Covariance Structure Models* by Long, No. 37 *Nonrecursive Causal Models* by Berry, No. 55 *The Logic of Causal Order* by Davis, and those numbers related to regression analysis in one way or another.

As Iacobucci describes in Chapter 2, there are three basic ways of dealing with mediation. The classical mediation test, originated in the 1980s, relies on classical linear regression. The directed acyclic graph approach uses paths and vertexes to present causal relations graphically and to model as such. Finally, the method known as structural equation modeling (SEM) offers the most flexibility in modeling mediation in causal analysis. This is the approach that Iacobucci took in writing the book, an approach that allows the researcher to deal with mediation in the presence of multiple measures, mediated moderation, and moderated mediation, among other variations on the mediation theme. The wide availability of software implementing SEM gives the reader necessary tools for modeling mediation so that a proper understanding of causal relationship is achieved.

— Tim F. Liao
Series Editor

ACKNOWLEDGMENTS

The author is grateful to Tim Liao (University of Illinois), James C. Anderson (Northwestern University), Rick Bagozzi (University of Michigan), Hans Baumgartner (Pennsylvania State University), Peter Bentler (UCLA), Joe Cote (Washington State University), Claes Fornell (University of Michigan), David Kenny (University of Connecticut), Don Lehmann (Columbia University), Robert MacCallum (University of North Carolina), Rod McDonald (University of Illinois), Richard Netemeyer (University of Virginia), and J. B. Steenkamp (University of North Carolina) for their helpful feedback.

MEDIATION ANALYSIS

Dawn Iacobucci
Owen Graduate School of Management, Vanderbilt University

CHAPTER 1. INTRODUCTION TO MEDIATION

Mediation analysis is a set of statistical procedures used to investigate whether a particular data set exhibits a mediational structure. A mediational structure posits a particular conceptualization of the mechanism through which an independent variable might affect a dependent variable—not directly, but rather through an intervening process, captured by the mediator variable. Researchers testing for mediation relationships usually make causal statements about these interrelationships, for example, that the independent variable *causes* or *affects* the mediator, which in turn *affects* the dependent variable. Researchers then test for the empirical relationships using a statistical methodological approach. In this book, we discuss both the conceptual and the statistical elements involved in examining mediation relationships.

In this chapter, we first review the logic of, and sociologically agreed on means of, establishing evidence for causality. These conceptual issues are relevant regardless of the particular statistical machinery (described subsequently) used to test mediation models.

In the mediation literature, some researchers have expressed renewed caution about the interpretation of causality in data structures that are usually correlational (e.g., Holland, 1986; James & Brett, 1984; James, Mulaik, & Brett, 1982; McDonald, 2002), some arguing that experimental methods still reign supreme in the establishment of causality (e.g., Shrout & Bolger, 2002; Spencer, Zanna, & Fong, 2005). Some researchers have tried to improve on the basic mediational statistical methods (e.g., Kenny, Kashy, & Bolger, 1998; MacKinnon, Lockwood, Hoffman, West, & Sheets, 2002; MacKinnon, Warsi, & Dwyer, 1995). And some researchers have tackled both the causal logical issues and the concerns regarding empirical improvements (e.g., Bentler, 2001; Cote, 2001; Lehmann, 2001; McDonald, 2001; Netemeyer, 2001). We will address all these topics.

2

1.1 What Is Mediation and Why Is It Important?

Mediation is of interest to many social science researchers (Baron & Kenny, 1986; Iacobucci, 2001; James & Brett, 1984; MacKinnon et al., 2002). A theoretical premise posits that an intervening variable is an indicative measure of the process through which an independent variable is thought to affect a dependent variable. The researcher seeks to assess the extent to which the effect of the independent variable on the dependent variable is direct or indirect via the mediator.

As depicted in Figure 1.1, X is the independent variable; M, the hypothesized mediator; and Y, the dependent variable. Traditionally, researchers study the relationship between predictor variables, such as X, and dependent variables, such as Y. In studies in which mediation is posited and tested, the question is whether the effect of X on Y is direct, $X \rightarrow Y$, or perhaps indirect, as mediated through variable M, that is, $X \rightarrow M \rightarrow Y$. Via the indirect path, the X variable is hypothesized to help predict and explain variability in the mediator M, which in turn is anticipated to help predict and explain variability in Y.

Underlying the quest for mediation is the motivation to understand the process by which X affects Y. After establishing some empirical phenomenon (i.e., X seems to affect Y), theory development advances by understanding the nature of that empirical finding; that is, how does X seem to affect Y? Perhaps the explanation is parsimonious: X explains some variability in Y, essentially on its own. Alternatively, perhaps X explains some variability in Y due to X's and Y's mutual relationship with an intervening variable, M.

Researchers seem to find the mediation logic intuitively appealing. One measure of the importance of mediation is the number of scholarly articles that incorporate mediation tests and logic, and indeed tests of mediation abound in numerous literatures. Here are just a few examples of recent applications:

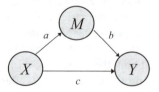

Figure 1.1 Simple, Standard Trivariate Mediation

NOTE: X = Independent variable; M = mediator; Y = dependent variable.

- X might be a trait (e.g., need for cognition); M, an attitude (e.g., toward an advertisement); and Y, a response judgment (e.g., likelihood to purchase the advertised item); alternatively,

- X could be a mood induction; M, a cognitive assessment; and Y, a recognition test of previously exposed stimuli; or perhaps

- X may be voter age; M, a scale of voters' political leanings (liberal to conservative); and Y, voting intentions.

- X could be a qualification of countries' economic development; M, an indicator of their movement toward democratic governance; and Y, the level of the countries' levels of prosperity.

- X may be a measure of individual risk-seeking tendencies; M, a rating of the riskiness of a particular financial vehicle; and Y, the propensity to invest in it.

- X might be a cultural measure (e.g., individualism); M, an index of fit between individual style and corporate culture; and Y, evidence of leadership. Finally, perhaps

- X is household income; M, a measure of school environment (e.g., facilitating autonomous learning); and Y, student performance on standardized tests.

The vast coverage of substantive topics in which mediation is a focus of investigation is one means of supporting the claim that mediation is important—it is popular. Regardless of the theoretical content, tests of mediation appeal to researchers attempting to track the process by which X is thought to affect Y.

We'll turn shortly to consider the methodology for testing for the presence of mediation: how mediation analyses are currently conducted, how they might be done better, what to do in tricky situations, and so on. However, first we review a few conceptual issues involving causality.

1.2 Causation

In this section, we review the necessary elements in presenting a case for causality. We do so because researchers conducting mediation tests frequently communicate their findings in causal language; for example, claiming that "X affects Y through M," or sometimes more explicitly, "X causes M, which in turn causes Y." It is nearly irresistible to interpret path models such as that in Figure 1.1 without stating or implying a causal chain from X to M to Y. In this discussion, we will acknowledge the challenges of establishing causality confidently with mediation techniques. To preview, the issues are two: First, the data used to test mediation analysis are usually correlational, and such data are limited in their capacity to yield clear conclusions regarding causality. Instead, many social science scholars hold the view that the mechanisms of manipulation and measurement used in experiments are still the best, and perhaps the only, method for detecting causality. Second, there is nothing inherent to any statistical technique that can imbue correlational data with causal meaning. Nevertheless, statements of causality are the goal for many researchers testing for mediation linkages, so the causality guidelines are important to understand, to enhance the likelihood that it might be established in any circumstance.

In attempting to establish evidence for causal relationships, philosophers of science largely converge on the criteria of Hume and Mills, necessitating (1) concomitant variation, (2) sequential ordering, and (3) elimination of rival explanations. We'll examine each.

1.2.1 Concomitant Variation

The principle of concomitant variation holds that if X causes Y, one would expect X and Y to be correlated. Social scientists study human behavior, which is notoriously subtle and complex, so even the satisfaction of this first requirement can be difficult.

There are several issues: First, there may be multiple causes; that is, X could be simply one of several causes of Y (e.g., household income would contribute to but not singularly determine automobile expenditures). Given the contextual complexities, the correlation between X and Y might be rather low, because additional factors help explain Y.

Second, if the theoretical premise holds in the population between the constructs X and Y, it is well-known that sampling and the operationalization and measurement of the indicator variables for X and Y all inevitably introduce random error. This error will attenuate the empirically observed relationship between the variables representing X and Y.

Third, if the correlation between two variables is weakened for any of these or other reasons, consider that the indirect path of interest in these mediation analyses is a chain of two probabilistic functions, involving r_{XM} and r_{MY}, hence further dampening the strength of the likely empirical findings in support of mediation path. That is, if all three paths are estimated with error, the single, direct link may appear more prominent, given that the indirect path, which involves two links, is muddied by error on both links.

Fourth, it would seem to be a perennial caution to social scientists to not overinterpret correlational data as indicative of causal relationships. The logic dictates: If there is a causal relationship, then there should be a correlational one. Even students in basic statistics are taught that the reverse is not necessarily true: Correlation does not imply causation. That is, X and Y can be correlated because $X \rightarrow Y$ or $Y \rightarrow X$ or a third variable gives rise to both X and Y, so the presence of a nonzero correlation does not point conclusively to any one of these three scenarios. This reminder is not unwarranted, given the prevalence of correlational data simultaneously with the causal summary statements by researchers presenting mediation analyses in published articles even in top journals. Baumrind (1983) is clear in her cautions that correlational data are not a basis for conclusive causal statements: "[We should] discourage the fantasy that any statistical system can justify drawing causal inferences from correlational data" (p. 1289). Breckler (1990) similarly states, "[correlational data do] not provide a sufficient basis for inferring causation" (p. 269).

The "micro" social sciences (e.g., consumer behavior, psychology, compared with sociology or macroeconomics) have the luxury of conducting experiments, universally acknowledged as the cleanest methodological device for identifying causal relationships (cf. Mill [2002] insisted on experimentation to establish causality with the key element being random assignment of observational units; also see Holland, 1988; Rubin, 1974, 2005). "The objective of the traditional . . . experiment is to enable the experimenter to infer unambiguously the existence and direction of causal relations" (Baumrind, 1983, p. 1290). Given that experimentation is a superior means of establishing causal links, Spencer et al. (2005) argue that the chain of causality ($X \rightarrow M \rightarrow Y$) should be tested in a series of experimental studies. Specifically, in the experimental framework, researchers would manipulate the independent variable X, and measure the impact on M, and in another study, M would be manipulated and its impact on Y measured.[1]

Occasionally, mediation analyses are conducted in the context of experimentation: An experiment is run, and the focal dependent variables are analyzed via analysis of variance (ANOVA). When researchers conduct even a simple 2×2 experiment and use ANOVA to test the results, the testing of a causal premise is as strong as it can be.[2] In terms of establishing causality, the experimenter should stop because that's as rigorous as a test can be. Adding a mediation analysis does not add to the rigor of the analyses, nor does it substantiate the confidence with which any conclusive causal statements can be made. Yet occasionally, after the ANOVA on the key dependent variables, researchers impute some supplemental measures into a mediation analysis. It is conceivable that researchers believe that they are adding value or rigor by introducing additional statistical tests (i.e., indices associated with running the mediation analyses), but it's not true—at least not in terms of establishing causal conclusions. When researchers tack on a mediation analysis, they are analyzing correlational data, which are never superior in identifying causal premises. Thus, the addition of mediation analyses after reporting ANOVAs on the central dependent variables dilutes, not strengthens, a paper. So a mediation analysis shouldn't be a knee-jerk addition to a researcher's analysis (nor a knee-jerk request of a reviewer).

With experimental data, the researcher has a strong logical basis for making claims of causality, $X \to M \to Y$ (e.g., Netemeyer, 2001); for studies with high internal validity, all the conditions are ceteris paribus except the manipulated factors, hence differences on dependent variables may be attributed cleanly to those experimental interventions. When instead mediation analyses are conducted on cross-sectional, correlational data, researchers must soften the language, making claims of "structural relationships" perhaps, but not "causality" (Holland, 1986; James et al., 1982).

1.2.2 Sequential Ordering

The principle of sequential ordering holds that if one seeks to establish that X causes Y, one would expect to see X occur prior to Y. This condition would seem simple enough to satisfy. Ideally, researchers would measure the variables in the order in which the processual mechanism is thought to operate: First X, then M, and then Y, not simply on subsequent pages of a survey but in three waves of data collection gathered at times t_1, t_2, and t_3. This procedure would allow for the investigation of the unfolding causal or temporal chain.[3] It might be the case that variables measured at t_1 have an impact (or not) on those measured at t_2, but it is clearly the case that variables measured at t_2 cannot have an impact on those measured at t_1. (Experiments unfold over time too; manipulations occur at t_1, and measured dependent variables at t_2, even if the duration between the two time points is brief.)

The goal of sequential ordering is achievable, that is, ideally having respondents complete survey items regarding X at t_1, M at t_2, and Y at t_3 (where the intermeasure durations are "nontrivial"). However, this ideal is rarely achieved for pragmatic reasons (logistics, participant mortality, etc.). Instead, most mediation tests are applied to correlational data measured in a cross-sectional design (i.e., data gathered at one time point). Furthermore, in the majority of published articles containing mediations, the measures of X, M, and Y are taken either simultaneously or out of order in one survey setting (e.g., usually Y being measured before M to keep the dependent variable pure, unaffected by other measurement or intervention). When all three measures are items or scales that appear on a single survey, the researcher bears the burden of arguing the ordered relationship on logical or theoretical grounds.

In some circumstances, this argument may be achievable, given that order might be less critical, for example, if X were a stable demographic or trait variable, it could be measured at the end of a survey without any concern of reactance; that is, that the measures of attitudes (M) or behaviors (Y) would have had an impact on the measure of a preexisting state, X.[4] Yet when X, M, and Y all comprise attitudinal measures, and they are taken out of order, it strains credulity regarding the conceptual arguments. Conversely, sequential ordering by itself is no panacea. If X were measured at time t_1, and M at t_2, and Y at t_3, it would nevertheless not do to make claims of a causal or temporal order, $X \rightarrow M \rightarrow Y$, if the constructs were, say, X = an attitude, M = a behavioral propensity, and Y = some individual trait or demographic characteristic, given that logically Y almost certainly existed prior to X or M. Even very sophisticated statistical tools cannot overcome weak logic.

In addition, the directionality of causal or temporal relationships may be difficult to establish, given that many nonrecursive relationships exist. Even if the majority of variance goes in the $X \rightarrow Y$ direction, it is not unusual to find some reciprocal effect, $X \leftarrow Y$. For example, marketers believe that advertising causes increased sales (i.e., advertising $\rightarrow$ sales), but usually advertising budgets are determined as a percentage of last year's sales (i.e., sales $\rightarrow$ advertising).

Finally, consider the fact that in many published articles containing mediation analyses, the M constructs are manipulation checks of an experimental intervention of X. A manipulation check indeed presumably inevitably follows the manipulation, yet no one would deem worthy a conceptual advance to the literature a mediation model that posits X to be some theoretical construct and M merely its measurement; nor would such a demonstration represent mediation as it is typically conceptualized.[5]

1.2.3 Elimination of Other Possible Explanations

Numerous classes of rival explanations have been documented, any of which could threaten the internal validity of the causal conclusion, that is, the certainty with which a researcher may conclude that the observed data patterns are indeed attributable to the theory being tested. For example, the marketer seeking to attribute a recent sales increase to a previous promotional effort must eliminate the possibility of a natural seasonal increase in sales (Churchill & Iacobucci, 2005). Once again, well-designed experiments are thought to be the most effective mechanism for "ruling out alternative causal explanations" (Baumrind 1983, p. 1290). Eliminating alternative explanations is a concern both simple and complex: Simple because it is a well-known goal, complex because its achievement is unknown. For example, McKim and Turner (1997) say that it is difficult to partial out potentially relevant variables, in part because we do not know all the possible causes. Mackie's (1974, 1980) INUS condition holds that perhaps at best we can identify a relationship between two variables for which the first variable is *Insufficient but Nonredundant (necessary) part of a condition that is Unnecessary but Sufficient* for the second variable. A frequent example poses the question, "Can we know whether a short circuit caused a house fire?" (cf. Suppes, 1970). Taking the second part ("unnecessary but sufficient") first, there are several conditions that could lead to a house fire; thus, a short circuit per se is unnecessary (a match could have started the fire) yet sufficient (certainly a short circuit can cause a house fire). Turning to the first part ("insufficient but nonredundant"), the short circuit alone is insufficient but necessary—other factors must also be present, for example, ignitable materials near the short circuit. Together, the INUS test tries to incorporate these conditions so as to make progress toward eliminating rival explanations.

The challenges in the logic and empirical testing are exacerbated in extended chains, for example, $X \to M_1 \to M_2 \to Y$ or models with multiple mediation paths, for example, $X \to M_1 \to Y$ and $X \to M_2 \to Y$ (Karson & Fisher, 2005; Salmon, 1997). Given the aforementioned issues of measurement error and sampling, it is important once again to acknowledge that these relationships are probabilistic. That is, one would seek to establish that the probability of the mediator occurring in the presence of the independent variable exceeds the likelihood that the mediator occurs in the absence of the independent variable, that is, $P(M|X) > P(M|{\sim}X)$ (and analogously for the relationship between the mediator and the dependent variable: $P(Y|M) > P(Y|{\sim}M)$), or as Sosa and Tooley (1993) suggest for the fuller chain, if $X \to M \to Y$, then $1.0 > P(Y|M) > P(Y|X) > P(Y) > 0.0$.

1.2.4 Mediation and Correlation and Causation

These problems of establishing causality are not new, of course. One means of shedding new light on this old problem may be to illustrate explicitly how a correlation matrix among the three focal constructs (X,

M, Y) can yield results consistent with the mediation structure posited in Figure 1.1, but also with a number of alternative competing models (cf. Breckler, 1990; Lee & Hershberger, 1990; MacCallum, Wegener, Uchino, & Fabrigar, 1993). We will treat the issues of model identification and model equivalence in greater detail later in this book (i.e., the conditions under which $X \rightarrow M$ cannot be distinguished from $X \leftarrow M$, etc.). For now, we might begin with Glymour's (2001, p. 33) observations that if we found variables X and Y to be uncorrelated conditional on M, specifically that the partial correlation between X and Y with M partialed out is zero ($r_{XY \cdot M} = 0$), such a result would be consistent with these models: (1) the traditional mediated model, $X \rightarrow M \rightarrow Y$; (2) one in which the entire directionality was reversed, $X \leftarrow M \leftarrow Y$; and (3) one in which M served as a common factor giving rise to X and Y, that is, $X \leftarrow M \rightarrow Y$.

Partial correlations offer a simple and precise language for the goals of a mediation test. Recall that a partial correlation, such as $r_{XY \cdot M}$, represents the extent to which X and Y are linearly related once M is accounted for in the relationships between X and M, and Y and M. Specifically, if $r_{XY \cdot M}$ = 0, it indicates that once M is partialed out, there is no remaining linear relationship between X and Y. Simon (1957, pp. 42–43) says that if we seek to test or support the model $X \rightarrow M \rightarrow Y$, we would expect that $r_{XY \cdot M} = 0$ or equivalently, $r_{XY} = (r_{XM})(r_{MY})$. (Given the probabilistic nature of data, $r_{XY \cdot M}$ might not equal zero precisely, so we would say that we would want $r_{XY \cdot M}$ to be nonsignificant; that is, not statistically significantly different from zero.) If the data support both the direct and the indirect paths, then the partial $r_{MY \cdot X}$ would be small but it would not vanish to zero or be nonsignificant (Asher, 1983, p. 21).

We will return to the issue of rival explanations and models. As a final observation about alternative theories, we can mention that it is the rare journal article in which the authors mention, much less test, a competing theory. It is perhaps a relatively more minor quibble to point out that rarely do the introduction sections of articles containing mediations mention that the research contained therein will examine the means by which X might influence Y, nor specifically that mediation tests will be conducted. Certainly, an introduction section of a book need not foreshadow all elements of the research inquiry; however, given the seemingly less than central role of the mediation question, the statistical tests typically appear to be post hoc—both theoretically and analytically an afterthought. This after-the-fact inclusion raises the conceptual question as to whether the mediation examination was necessary, and certainly the statistical concern of capitalizing on chance in the post hoc tests.

Notes

1. Spencer, Zanna, and Fong (2005) say that the only possible concern is if the mediator is easier to measure than manipulate. Note, however, that this should not be a problem if the measured and manipulated variants of the mediator are purportedly tapping the same theoretical construct.

2. This is not to say that studies cannot be designed with flaws, but when true, the mediation analysis would be as problematic as the analysis of variance.

3. Breckler (1990) says that "cross-sectional data clearly do not justify causal inferences" and that "longitudinal data provide a stronger basis [for establishing evidence of causality]." Even so, "other criteria are typically required to firmly support a causal conclusion" (p. 269).

4. Davis (1985, p. 15) refers to good candidates for precursors, such as Xs in mediations, as those respondent characteristics that are "relatively sticky," including religious preference, occupational prestige, income, region of residence, political party identification, IQ, marital status, number of children in the household, and so on. Good candidate variables for Ms or Ys would be those that are "relatively loose" or mutable, such as indicators of happiness, media-viewing habits, brand preferences, and general attitudes.

5. A manipulation check serving as M would seem to not satisfy commonly understood definitions of mediation, for example, James and Brett (1984), defining mediation: "M is a mediator of the probabilistic relations $Y = f(X)$ if M is a probabilistic function of M (i.e., $Y = f(M)$), where X, M and Y *have different ontological content (i.e., represent different hypothetical constructs or latent variables)* [italics added]" (p. 310).

CHAPTER 2. MEDIATION ANALYSIS BASICS

In this chapter, we describe the methods of testing for empirical evidence of mediation. We begin by briefly reviewing the traditional regression-based approach for testing mediation patterns, per Baron and Kenny (1986) and the Sobel (1982) follow-up z test. The methods offer criteria for researchers to claim the presence of "full," "partial," or "no" mediation in their data. We'll discuss how to execute the techniques properly, pitfalls to avoid, and controversies in the literature.

We then consider the possibility of an alternative approach examining mediation structures via directed acyclic graphs. This approach is useful conceptually, but empirically the remaining approach—that of structural equations modeling (SEM)—will prove to be superior in examining mediation and its many extensions. Thus, after briefly reviewing the regression and graph approaches, the remainder of the book is built on the SEM foundation.

2.1   The Classic Mediation Test

The most popular means of testing for mediation is the procedure offered by Baron and Kenny (1986). Using their approach, the researcher fits three regression models:

$$M = \beta_1 + aX + \varepsilon_1, \qquad\qquad [2.1]$$

$$Y = \beta_2 + cX + \varepsilon_2, \qquad\qquad [2.2]$$

$$Y = \beta_3 + c'X + bM + \varepsilon_3, \qquad\qquad [2.3]$$

where the βs (betas) are the intercepts (which are ignored), the εs (epsilons) are the model fit errors (which are also largely ignored), and the a, b, c, and c' terms are the regression coefficients capturing the relationships between the three focal variables. Evidence for mediation is said to be likely if

1. the term a in Equation 2.1 is significant; that is, there is evidence of a linear relationship between the independent variable (X) and the mediator (M);

2. the regression coefficient c in Equation 2.2 is significant; there is a linear relationship between the independent variable (X) and the dependent variable (Y)[1]; and

3. the term b in Equation 2.3 is significant, indicating that the mediator (M) helps predict the dependent variable (Y), and also c', the effect of

the independent variable (X) directly on the dependent variable (Y), becomes significantly smaller in size relative to c in Equation 2.2.

The last criterion, the comparison of size between c in Equation 2.2 and c' in Equation 2.3, is conducted by the z test (Sobel, 1982).[2] It can be shown that testing the difference between c (the direct effect), and c' (the direct effect estimated while controlling for the indirect, mediated effect) is equivalent to testing whether the strength of the mediated path ($a \times b$) exceeds zero:

$$z = \frac{a \times b}{\sqrt{b^2 s_a^2 + a^2 s_b^2}}, \qquad [2.4]$$

where a and s_a^2 are obtained from Equation 2.1, and b and s_b^2 from 2.3.[3-5]

Note that regression weights, bs, can be used, or standardized regression weights, βs, as long as their appropriate respective standard errors are also used. Recall $SE\left(\beta_X\right) = \left(s_X / s_Y\right) SE\left(b_X\right)$, $SE\left(\beta_M\right) = \left(s_M / s_Y\right) SE\left(b_M\right)$, or $SE\left(b_X\right) = \left(s_Y / s_X\right) SE\left(\beta_X\right)$ and $SE\left(b_M\right) = \left(s_Y / s_M\right) SE\left(\beta_M\right)$.

If a is not significant, or b is not significant (and certainly if neither is significant), there is said to be no mediation; and the researcher concludes that all the variance in Y attributable to X is direct, not mediated through M, and stops the analysis. If (1), (2), and (3) hold, the researcher would conclude there is (at least) "partial" mediation; the variance in Y attributable to X is partly a direct effect, and partly an indirect effect mediated through M. If (1), (2), and (3) hold, and c' is not significantly different from zero, the effect is said to be perfect or complete mediation; all the variance in Y explained by X is indirect, mediated through M.[6, 7]

It is not unusual for research articles to underreport analytical details, but even giving the underrepresentation in the journals the benefit of the doubt, many mediation analyses are conducted incorrectly. For example, while the analyses in the majority of articles follow steps (1) through (3) properly, not all do. Furthermore, most do not report the z test.[8] When all tests are properly conducted and reported, the majority of articles conclude with "partial mediation" as the result. While this status seems to be a sensible benchmark, that is, some of the variance in Y explained by X is direct, and some is indirect through the mechanism M, it is nevertheless a somewhat unexciting result.

The Baron and Kenny (1986) article has been enormously influential both in shaping how researchers think about mediation and in providing procedures to detect mediation patterns in data.[9] In addition to users applying the techniques for their own substantive and theoretical research inquiries, methodological research has also been fostered, in which researchers investigate a number of concerns about the empirical behavior of the mediation tests and its components.[10] For example, MacKinnon and his colleagues have conducted methodological tests comparing alternative statistics with respect to their relative power in detecting mediation patterns, as well as the comparative utility of rival indices expressing the extent to which a mediation structure is present in data (MacKinnon et al., 1995, 2002).[11]

2.2   An Alternative: Directed Acyclic Graphs

There is a remarkably healthy literature at the nexus of philosophy of science, statistics and machine learning converging on examining causality (cf. Hayduk et al. (2003); McKim & Turner, 1997; Pearl, 2000; Salmon, 1997). These scholars are reconsidering the logic of causal concepts as well as the means of examining and determining manifest empirical relationships (e.g., Shafer, 1996; Spirtes, Glymour, & Scheines, 2001). Given the renewed acknowledgement of the complexities, some are referring to the "art" of establishing cause and effect (cf. McDonald, 2002; Pearl, 2000). One tool many of these researchers are using is "directed acyclical graphs" or DAGs, which appear quite relevant to the question of mediation.

The terms are defined as follows: A *graph* is composed of links (e.g., causal or correlational relationships) and nodes (e.g., variables such as X, M, and Y). A graph is *directed* when the links originate from one node (e.g., X) and are relationally tied toward another (e.g., Y). A directed graph is certainly *acyclical* if the graph is nonrecursive (as per mediations) or if the ends of a causal chain do not redirect toward sources of variance. That is, a link cannot return to any originating node. (In contrast, examples of a cyclical graph would be $X \to M \to Y \dashrightarrow X$, or $X \to M \to Y \to M$.)

If the relationship between X and Y were fully mediated, DAG analysts would say that conditional on M, X and Y are independent. DAG notation would posit that the probability of X given Y and M may be equated to the conditional probability of the presence or strength of X given M. Specifically, if $P(X \mid Y, Z) = P(X \mid Z)$, then $X \perp Y \mid M$. Empirically these probabilities could be estimated, and this relationship estimated via the computation of the partial $r_{XY \cdot M}$. If the partial is not significant (different from zero), the independence relationship would hold. Presumably, if $P(X \mid Y, Z) \neq P(X \mid Z)$, then there is some lesser extent of mediation ("partial mediation" or "no mediation," with no means of distinguishing these cases).

DAGs provide a relevant theoretical framework; that is, the $X \to M \to Y$ mediation inquiry is certainly a directed acyclic graph. However, McKim and Turner (1997) point out that DAGs do not answer the question of how to infer causation from associative data (or, correlations), and Humphreys and Freedman (1996) argue that these techniques do not uncover causal structure but rather assume the causality.

In addition, DAGs aren't that useful empirically in the mediation quest, and to be fair, nor were they intended to be so. For example, there is DAG software, but its goal is to discover the DAGs in the data (Haughton, Kamis, & Scholten, 2006; Shipley, 2000). Locating DAGs can be useful in complex networks, with many nodes and interconnections, where patterns are difficult to visually discern, identifying recursive chains and separating them from loops and cycles. However, this pursuit is not relevant in mediation analysis—we know where the DAG is (and there are usually very few nodes, indeed often only three). There are DAG techniques (e.g., "D-separation," a focus on particular paths within the model), which are similar to estimating partial correlations, and yet which afford the technique no advantage over structural equations (Hayduk et al., 2003). For example, Pearl (2001) discusses how to decompose a $X \rightarrow M \rightarrow Y$ chain into direct and indirect effects, but structural equations modeling does that as well. No extensions to the basic mediation model are programmed or accessible in the popular computing packages, and there are no goodness-of-fit indices. Thus, the DAG approach would not provide an optimal means of analyzing mediational data.

2.3 A Superior Alternative: Structural Equations Models

The greatest methodological advance in the mediation literature is clearly the movement toward encouraging scholars to test for mediation patterns using the SEM. The regression techniques are easy to conduct, and they were fine for the Baron and Kenny (1986) article, but researchers frequently encounter scenarios that are more complicated, and they need guidance. In addition, SEM itself has grown in accessibility and popularity and is a tool well-suited for testing for evidence of mediation patterns in data.

For example, consider a scenario in which a researcher has multiple indicators of the X, M, and/or Y constructs. (This situation was prefigured by Baron and Kenny in 1986, but not addressed fully in their article.) SEM offers the perfect blend of a measurement model and a structural model; the first, to enhance the reliability of the measured constructs, the second, to examine the possibly mediational interrelationships among the constructs.

Second, consider a scenario in which the X, M, and Y constructs are themselves embedded in a richer nomological network that contains additional antecedent and/or consequential constructs. The typical regression user is somewhat at a loss as to how to proceed in testing the focal $X \rightarrow M \rightarrow Y$ mediation in the presence of other constructs; for example, in which of the Equations 2.1 to 2.3 do the other constructs serve as predictors, when would the additional constructs serve as dependent variables, what parameter estimates are then compared, and so on.

A specific sort of extended nomological network would be one that tests for multiple mediator paths, for example, $X \to M_1 \to Y$ and $X \to M_2 \to Y$, or causal chains longer than the traditional, for example, $X \to M_1 \to M_2 \to Y$. The extension of a regression approach to answering these questions is not obvious, but the extension within SEM is straightforward, as we shall demonstrate.

Thus, in this book, we illustrate the SEM tests for mediation, beginning with the simplest mediation structure, adding a measurement model, and then adding complexities to the structural model. We will also use the techniques to revisit other issues, including testing for moderated mediation.

Notes

1. This path, $X \to Y$, is intuitively appealing, that is, addressing the question, "Is there any variance in Y explained by X, whether it will be shown to be indirect or direct?" However, since 1986, this criterion has become somewhat controversial, with critics arguing that should the mediation be complete, for example, all variance going from X to Y through M (or multiple Ms), then the direct path may be properly insignificant. For more on this issue, see James, Mulaik, and Brett (2007); Kenny, Kashy, and Bolger (1998); and Shrout and Bolger (2002).

2. The Sobel (1982) z test is important, because Step 3 of Baron and Kenny (1986) is either widely misunderstood or misapplied. The question is whether the parameter estimate c' in Equation 2.3, that is, the strength of the direct path from X to Y in the presence of M, is significantly smaller than c in Equation 2.2 (the equation without M). The goal is to show that c' is "significantly less" than c. This goal is not to be mistaken for showing that c' is "less significant" than c had been. Many researchers make the latter mistake—they provide the estimate for c, its t value, and some p value, say 0.05, then provide the analogous information for c', with p values that might be, say, 0.13 and conclude, "See, c' is less significant than c." That result is irrelevant. The first parameter c could be significant(ly greater than 0), say $c = .25$, and c' might be not significant(ly different from 0), say $c' = .10$, but c' might not be significantly less than c. The z test is a direct test of whether .10 (c) is less than .25 (c').

3. A term is added in the denominator by Baron and Kenny for the "population" formula (1986; i.e., $z = (a \times b) / \sqrt{b^2 s_a^2 + a^2 s_b^2 + s_a^2 s_b^2}$), and subtracted by Goodman for the "sample estimate" (1960; i.e., $z = (a \times b) / \sqrt{b^2 s_a^2 + a^2 s_b^2 - s_a^2 s_b^2}$). Given that s_a^2 and s_a^2 are variances, their product $s_a^2 s_b^2 > 0$. Hence, the former test is conservative, the latter more powerful. Accordingly, the middling Sobel test, $z = (a \times b) / \sqrt{b^2 s_a^2 + a^2 s_b^2}$, has been described as easy to defend and a good approximation especially in large samples. In any event, these variances (s_a^2 and s_b^2) of the parameter estimates are typically small (e.g., 0.02), producing a product that is negligible (e.g., .004—teeny times teeny equals even teenier).

4. Mediation implies the presence of an indirect path. Complete mediation would also imply the diminution of the direct path. Partial mediation would exist in the coexisting presence of a direct and indirect path.

5. MacKinnon et al. (2002) have pointed out that this test can be underpowered (i.e., somewhat too conservative) and are working on creating asymmetric confidence intervals to compensate and improve the estimates.

6. It has been suggested that rather than summarizing mediation analyses as one of three categorical results (i.e., no mediation, partial mediation, or full mediation), it would be more informative to create a continuous index of the proportion of the variance in Y due to the indirect mediated path (Lehmann, 2001; MacKinnon, Warsi, & Dwyer, 1995), $ab/(ab + c)$.

7. One debate in the literature regarding the proper assessments of mediation that researchers point to is the condition given in Equation 2.1, that X is a significant predictor of M, which implies that there will always be multicollinearity between X and M when they are used jointly to predict Y in Equation 2.3. Due to the presence of this multicollinearity, these researchers argue that it is conceptually and statistically difficult to separate the effects of X and M on Y via the regression weights, and hence, the change in R^2s assessing the fits of models 2.2 and 2.3 should be compared and tested (e.g., Cote, 2001; Lehmann, 2001). Unfortunately, there are also legitimate criticisms against using R^2s to assess the comparisons between models. In particular, such assessments of total variance accounted for at the omnibus model level do not precisely ascribe where the relationships among the variables are strong. R^2 information is diagnostic just for overall patterns, and is too macro to be useful. Baron and Kenny (1986) also raise the concern that the multicollinearity results in reduced power in testing the coefficients in Equation 2.3.

8. Preacher and Hayes (2004) ask quite pointedly, why is it the case that significance tests of the indirect effects in mediation are not conducted more frequently? For researchers uncertain as to how to compute such tests, MacKinnon et al. (2002) offer a highly comprehensive source (see their table 1).

9. For example, see Mattanah, Hancock & Brand (2004). Mediations are so frequently run, they are now serving as the foundation in meta-analyses (e.g., Shadish, 1996).

10. For example, some researchers are exploring the use of bootstrapping (techniques that make no distributional assumptions; cf. MacKinnon, Lockwood, & Williams, 2004), especially for small samples (because statistics based on assumptions of multivariate normality tends to hold asymptotically, that is, for very large samples; cf. Preacher & Hayes, 2006). MacKinnon, Warsi, and Dwyer (1995) found estimates of mediated effects fairly well-behaved for sample sizes of only 50 (or greater), except they urge larger samples ($n > 500$) when the independent variable is dichotomized (thus the classic finding of losing information when making a continuous variable binary, resulting in a more conservative test, and the data need to be fortified with larger n).

11. Also see www.public.asu.edu/~davidpm/ripl/mediate.htm.

CHAPTER 3. MEDIATION WITH STRUCTURAL EQUATIONS MODELING: THE MEASUREMENT MODEL

SEM is a state-of-the-art and powerful statistical approach that allows researchers to study mediation relationships in a wider array of contexts. Structural equations models integrate a measurement model and a structural model. In this chapter, we examine the measurement part of the structural equations model. We'll consider the extension of mediation models to include multiple indicators of any of the constructs. In the following chapter, we examine the structural part of the structural equations model. There we will then examine the model extensions required as more constructs are considered simultaneously with X, M, and Y.

3.1 Mediation in the Presence of Multiple Measures

Social science data subjected to mediation analysis are usually obtained from human respondents and thus estimations of statistical relationships will be attenuated due to measurement error. Baron and Kenny (1986, p. 1177) acknowledge that, like any regression, their basic approach makes no particular allowance for measurement error, which is simply subsumed into the overall error term, contributing to the lack of fit, $1 - R^2$. While it is true that proceeding with a single variable as a sole indicator of a construct is statistically conservative, most social scientists concur in the view that multi-item scales are generally preferable, in philosophical accordance with classical test theory and notions of reliability that more items comprise a stronger measurement instrument.[1] The 1986 regression procedures are applicable only to systems of three variables, that is, only one indicator measure per each of the three constructs, yet Figure 3.1 illustrates a typical research investigation that provides for multi-item scales for each of the focal constructs. The figure is merely an example; for the techniques to be described, the number of items may be two or more, for each of X, M, and Y.

It is perhaps easiest to envision the scenario in which there exist multiple predictor variables, X_1, X_2, X_3, and a single mediator M and a single dependent variable Y. In the regression context, Equations 2.1 to 2.3 would be replaced with the variants containing the multiple predictor variables:

$$M = \beta_4 + a_1 X_1 + a_2 X_2 + a_3 X_3 + \varepsilon_4 , \qquad [3.1]$$

$$Y = \beta_5 + c_1 X_1 + c_2 X_2 + c_3 X_3 + \varepsilon_5 , \qquad [3.2]$$

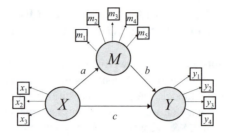

Figure 3.1   Multi-Item Scales for Three Constructs

$$Y = \beta_6 + c_1'X_1 + c_2'X_2 + c_3'X_3 + bM + \varepsilon_6. \qquad [3.3]$$

However, even in this simple extension, the complicating issues become two: First, it is not clear which coefficients should be compared to assess the extent of mediation, and second, the effects of the multicollinearity among X_1, X_2, X_3, which is inherent to predictors that represent multiple indicators of a common construct, would be debilitating.

The scenario becomes even more complex should the mediator M or the dependent variable Y be measured with more than one item. At first, it might seem that the new complexities would be simply analogous to those for X. However, M and Y each serve as dependent variables in the series of mediation regressions, hence a proliferation of Ms or Ys would require more predictive equations; for example, three mediators and two dependent variables would yield

$$M_1 = \beta_7 + a_1X_1 + a_2X_2 + a_3X_3 + \varepsilon_7, \qquad [3.4]$$

$$M_2 = \beta_8 + a_1X_1 + a_2X_2 + a_3X_3 + \varepsilon_8, \qquad [3.5]$$

$$M_3 = \beta_9 + a_1X_1 + a_2X_2 + a_3X_3 + \varepsilon_9, \qquad [3.6]$$

$$Y_1 = \beta_{10} + c_1X_1 + c_2X_2 + c_3X_3 + \varepsilon_{10}, \qquad [3.7]$$

$$Y_2 = \beta_{11} + c_1X_1 + c_2X_2 + c_3X_3 + \varepsilon_{11}, \qquad [3.8]$$

$$Y_1 = \beta_{12} + c_1'X_1 + c_2'X_2 + c_3'X_3 + bM_1 + \varepsilon_{12}, \qquad [3.9]$$

$$Y_1 = \beta_{13} + c_1'X_1 + c_2'X_2 + c_3'X_3 + bM_2 + \varepsilon_{13}, \qquad [3.10]$$

$$Y_1 = \beta_{14} + c_1' X_1 + c_2' X_2 + c_3' X_3 + b M_3 + \varepsilon_{14},$$ [3.11]

$$Y_2 = \beta_{15} + c_1' X_1 + c_2' X_2 + c_3' X_3 + b M_1 + \varepsilon_{15},$$ [3.12]

$$Y_2 = \beta_{16} + c_1' X_1 + c_2' X_2 + c_3' X_3 + b M_2 + \varepsilon_{16},$$ [3.13]

$$Y_2 = \beta_{17} + c_1' X_1 + c_2' X_2 + c_3' X_3 + b M_3 + \varepsilon_{17}.$$ [3.14]

Even with this modest extension to just a few measured variables for each of the three constructs, the number of equations and combinations for testing has increased greatly. The mediation analyst has two options. First, most researchers would compute means over the items within each scale, that is, X_1, X_2, X_3, to form $\overline{X}$, and so on. With the constructs represented by these aggregates, the measurement scenario is simplified, and the model closely parallels Equations 2.1 to 2.3, namely,

$$\overline{M} = \beta_{18} + a\overline{X} + \varepsilon_{18},$$ [3.15]

$$\overline{Y} = \beta_{19} + c\overline{X} + \varepsilon_{19},$$ [3.16]

$$\overline{Y} = \beta_{20} + c'\overline{X} + b\overline{M} + \varepsilon_{20}.$$ [3.17]

Hence, a multivariate problem has effectively been reduced to simpler univariate predictions. We will show momentarily that this solution is acceptable but not optimal.

3.2 Mediation and the Measurement Model of Structural Equations Models

The second option is to use structural equations models. Structural equations models are designed precisely for the task of solving systems of linear equations such as Equations 3.4 through 3.14. SEM is commonplace in the social sciences; the software is accessible, and the logic widely understood (Kline, 1998). SEM provides the state-of-the-art approach to test for mediated relationships among constructs particularly when multiple items or variables have been measured to capture any of the focal constructs.[2] Brown (1997) and Long (2006) are superb primers.

Table 3.1 depicts the generalization of the basic mediation inquiry to those situations in which X, M, or Y are measured with multi-item scales. The table represents all combinations of single versus multiple measures of X, M, and Y. It illustrates the conditions for which a regression approach may be used. Specifically, the regression technique may be applied any time each of the X, M, and Y constructs is represented by a single score, whether a single variable (e.g., M) or a scale composed of the average of the items purporting to measure the construct (e.g., $\{M_1, M_2, M_3\} \rightarrow \bar{M}$). More generally, however, SEM may be used in any scenario, and it is the only technique applicable in most of the scenarios. Even in the simplest data scenario where a regression might seem to provide an alternative, we will demonstrate that even though there is some correspondence between the regression and SEM approaches, the SEM technique is the superior method on both theoretical and empirical statistical grounds.

TABLE 3.1

Analyses Permissible Given Specific Data Properties:
Structural Equations Models and Regressions

Number of Mediator (M) Measures[a]	Number of Independent Variable (X) Measures[a]	Number of Dependent Variable (Y) Measures[a]		
		One Dependent Measure	Multiple Dependent Measures	One Aggregate Dependent Measure
		Y	Y_1, Y_2, Y_3	$\bar{Y}$
M	X	SEM, Reg[b, c]	SEM	SEM, Reg[c]
	X_1, X_2, X_3	SEM	SEM	SEM
	$\bar{X}$	SEM, Reg[c]	SEM	SEM, Reg[c]
M_1, M_2, M_3	X	SEM	SEM	SEM
	X_1, X_2, X_3	SEM	SEM	SEM
	$\bar{X}$	SEM	SEM	SEM
$\bar{M}$	X	SEM, Reg[c]	SEM	SEM, Reg[c]
	X_1, X_2, X_3	SEM	SEM	SEM
	$\bar{X}$	SEM, Reg[c]	SEM	SEM, Reg[c]

NOTES: Structural equations models (SEM) are always appropriate. Regressions (Reg) cannot be used if any construct is measured with multiple items (not captured as a single mean).

a. Where three measures are depicted (e.g., M_1, M_2, M_3), it is important to note that the multi-item measurement principles illustrated in this monograph also hold for two or four or more items.

b. This scenario depicts the classic mediation analysis, involving a single measure for each construct X, M, and Y.

c. These eight cells represent scenarios for which only a single measure (e.g., M) or scale (e.g., $\bar{M}$) is modeled.

In sum, the table shows that structural equations models are always appropriate. Regressions cannot be used if any construct is measured with multiple items (not captured as a single mean). Thus, in any scenario in Table 3.1, SEM provides the natural choice and the most appropriate technique for examining mediation structures.

3.3 Illustration

We have been arguing that the SEM approach is statistically theoretically superior to a series of regressions. In this section, we demonstrate this superiority with a few illustrative data sets and analyses. First, let's compare the performance of structural equations models and regressions in the simplest data scenario of one X, one M, and one Y variable representing each of their respective constructs (the first cell in Table 3.1). In this (and only this) simplest of scenarios, we will see that the techniques yield some similar results, but we will also track the differences between the regression and SEM approaches.

The equations that derive the path coefficients from the correlations are as follows (Asher, 1983; James et al., 1982):

$$a = r_{XM},$$

$$b = \left(\frac{1}{1-r_{XM}^2}\right)\left(r_{MY} - r_{XM}r_{XY}\right),$$

$$c = \left(\frac{1}{1-r_{XM}^2}\right)\left(r_{XY} - r_{XM}r_{MY}\right). \qquad [3.18]$$

The obverse equations for deriving the correlations from path coefficients are as follows:

$$r_{XM} = a,$$

$$r_{XY} = c + ab,$$

$$r_{MY} = b + ac. \qquad [3.19]$$

Say a researcher is working with the correlation matrix: $r_{XM} = 0.55$, $r_{XY} = 0.45$, $r_{MY} = 0.63$. From these correlations, we use Equations 3.18 to estimate the path coefficients a, b, c (representing $X \rightarrow M$, $M \rightarrow Y$, and $X \rightarrow Y$, respectively) to be $a = 0.55$, $b = 0.55$, and $c = 0.15$. These path coefficients indicate that two thirds of the variance in Y explained by X is indirect through the mediator M, that is,

$$\frac{\hat{a} \times \hat{b}}{(\hat{a} \times \hat{b}) + \hat{c}} = \frac{0.55 \times 0.55}{(0.55 \times 0.55) + 0.15} = 66.9\% \,.$$

In this simplest of data scenarios, that is, only three constructs, and only one measure representing each construct, the estimated path coefficients are identical whether computed via regression or SEM. Each technique bases the parameter estimates on Equations 3.18.

And yet the techniques differ systematically in an important way. The standard errors of the coefficients are larger for the regression approach than for the SEM. For the regressions, based on a modest sample of $n = 50$, $SE(a) = 0.121$, $SE(b) = 0.134$, $SE(c) = 0.134$. For SEM, $SE(a) = 0.119$, $SE(b) = 0.131$, $SE(c) = 0.131$. The differences are small (and to be fair, they get smaller with larger n), but systematic. Smaller standard errors are desirable statistically, indicative of greater precision in the estimation and hence are preferred.

This advantage of SEM over regression is due to the fact that the standard errors in the SEM approach are reduced, because of the simultaneous estimation of all parameters in the structural equations model. Fitting three separate regression models introduces biases due to missing variables. Instead, modeling all relationships simultaneously in one model is always statistically superior to doing so in a piecemeal fashion in separate models, because the model estimation is able to statistically control for and partial out other relationships. Thus, the empirical results just shown are not a coincidence, nor a function of the particular data example; rather, they are driven by the statistical theory that the simultaneously fit equations will dominate in producing more consistent estimates. Both theoretically and empirically, fitting a single SEM model lends more efficient and elegant estimation than the three regression pieces. And given the smaller standard errors in maximum likelihood SEM compared with ordinary least squares regressions, it should be no surprise that z test for the presence of mediation is "uniformly most powerful" (another statistically optimal quality) for SEM than regression.

In fitting one simultaneous model, all the parameters and standard errors (pieces of the z test) are estimated conditional on the same effects being present in the model. The effects of each of $X \rightarrow M$, $X \rightarrow Y$, and $M \rightarrow Y$ are estimated within the same modeling context, compared with the regression modeling, in which $X \rightarrow M$ and $X \rightarrow Y$ are first estimated with no other effects in the model, which makes them neither comparable to each other nor comparable to the fuller $\{X, M\} \rightarrow Y$ model. Currently, the z test is formed after deriving estimates from different regression models, for which the estimates are based on conditioning on different subsets of predictor variables. That is, in sum, the regression approach compares apples and oranges; the structural equations model compares apples and apples.

The smaller standard errors drive the result found in recent research comparing the SEM and regression analytical approaches employing a series of Monte Carlo simulations (Iacobucci, Saldanha, & Deng, 2007). The strength of simulation studies is that the population parameters are constructed and known, so the researcher is certain about the true relationship in a population, and the logic is to investigate the extent to which the regressions or structural equation models are capable of identifying and recovering it properly. The results document that SEM is more powerful than regression for all sample sizes, with the greatest differences between the techniques favoring SEM especially for small samples ($n = 30$), when the researcher can benefit from the additional compensatory power of the test. The SEM methodology was also superior in identifying mediation structures for all patterns of intercorrelations among the constructs, with greatest advantage for data with proportionally strong mediation effects (e.g., 75% and 100% mediation), when the researcher would be particularly expectant to detect such effects.[3, 4]

Thus, even in this simplest of data scenarios—the classic case of only three constructs and only one measure per construct—the choice between regression and structural equations models matters, and SEM is the superior technology. The SEM results work to the researcher's benefit, in being more likely to detect existing patterns of mediation, being truer to the known population structural characteristics, and in being statistically more defensible, given the elegance of the simultaneous estimation. Finally, as we shall now demonstrate, SEM allows researchers to examine mediation in scenarios where the application of regression would be difficult or impossible.

3.4 Fitting the Measurement Model

Next, we consider the conceptual and practical issues of fitting the measurement model to data. First, the three-variable model is discussed, then multiple measures are introduced, then the LISREL syntax is offered and explained.

3.4.1 How to Fit the Basic Three-Variable Mediation via SEM

When SEM is the tool used for mediation analyses, one model is fit. The paths from $X \rightarrow M$, $X \rightarrow Y$, and $M \rightarrow Y$ are all estimated simultaneously

The researcher does not fit a series of equations or models per the regression techniques. The single structural equations model follows:

$$Y = \Gamma X + BY + \Psi.$$ [3.20]

The X is called an exogenous variable, and M and Y are both included in Equation 3.20 under "Y," and they're called endogenous variables (basically X has no variable as a precursor, whereas both M and Y have one or more variables leading to them via $\rightarrow$). Of central interest in a mediation analysis are the structural parameters, Γ and B. Those matrices take the following forms:

$$\Gamma = \begin{matrix} \\ M \\ Y \end{matrix} \begin{matrix} X \\ \left[\begin{matrix} \gamma_{MX} \\ \gamma_{YX} \end{matrix} \right] \end{matrix}, \quad \rightarrow \quad B = \begin{matrix} \\ M \\ Y \end{matrix} \begin{matrix} M \qquad\qquad Y \\ \left[\begin{matrix} \beta_{MM} = 0 & \beta_{MY} = 0 \\ \beta_{YM} & \beta_{YY} = 0 \end{matrix} \right] \end{matrix}$$

In Γ, the exogenous variable (or construct, as the mapping is perfect in the three variable case) forms the column, and its effects on the endogenous rows M and Y are the terms, γ_{MX} and γ_{YX}, respectively.[5] The B matrix is mostly full of zeros (i.e., corresponding to paths that are not estimated, e.g., $Y \rightarrow M$), but one term, β_{YM} is estimated, and it represents the path $M \rightarrow Y$. We will elaborate on the interpretation of these Γ and B terms shortly, but for completion, we also mention that a Ψ matrix is estimated, which contains the endogenous models' lack of fit, essentially, $1 - R^2$ for trying to predict M and Y:

$$\Psi = \begin{matrix} \\ M \\ Y \end{matrix} \begin{matrix} M \quad\; Y \\ \left[\begin{matrix} \psi_M & 0 \\ 0 & \psi_Y \end{matrix} \right] \end{matrix}.$$

Returning to the important structural parameters, a significant $X \rightarrow Y$ path (i.e., the γ_{YX} estimate) would suggest that at least some of the variance in Y is explained by a direct relationship with X, that the inclusion of a mediator does not alone sufficiently support the process by which X has an impact on Y (and in fact, the mediated path may not be necessary). If both the $X \rightarrow M$ and $M \rightarrow Y$ paths are significant (i.e., γ_{MX} and β_{YM}, respectively), then at least some of the variance in Y is explained by an indirect, mediated relationship with X through M. If only one of the two indirect paths ($X \rightarrow M$ or $M \rightarrow Y$) is significant, the mediated path logic may hold promise for future research (e.g., perhaps the nonsignificant path was measured with unreliable instruments or the study was conducted with an insufficient sample size), but the results preclude a mediation conclusion in the current study.

If both the $X \to M$ and $M \to Y$ paths coefficients are significant, then the researcher should conduct the follow-up z test. This follow-up test is still important in the SEM approach because whether $X \to Y$ is significant or not, the question is one of assessing the size of the mediated path compared with that of the direct path. Say the estimates were 0.7 for $X \to M$, 0.6 for $M \to Y$, and 0.3 for $X \to Y$, and say the first two were significant and the third was not. Qualitatively, it might appear that a hypothesis for mediation is supported, over a hypothesis of a direct link. However, those significance tests would indicate merely that 0.7 and 0.6 each were greater than 0.0, and that 0.3 was not. The indirect paths might not be significantly greater than the direct path. That is, 0.7 may not be significantly greater than 0.3, and certainly the indirect path product, 0.7×0.6, may not be greater than 0.3. The z test compares directly whether the mediated path (0.7×0.6) exceeds the strength of the direct path (0.3).

While the form of the z test is the same as that in Equation 2.4, the advantage of the SEM is that all the components in the test, both the estimates a and b and their standard errors s_a and s_b, are obtained from the same model 3.20. Hence, every estimate is derived while partialling out all the same set of other effects, making each estimate as unbiased as possible, essentially grounding them all on the same footing.

To be useful, we will translate these statistical and matrix concepts into software commands, for the reader who wishes to implement structural equations models for their mediation tests. We now present the LISREL syntax for running each model we posit, because LISREL is probably the most popular of the SEM software packages.[6] We provide syntax for fitting the basic mediation models via other popular packages (SAS's PROC CALIS, EQS, and AMOS) in the Appendix. While we walk through the syntax, we do so succinctly, assuming a bit of familiarity with LISREL (Jöreskog & Sörbom, 1997). We begin by illustrating the LISREL syntax to run the simple three-variable analysis (a trivariate mediation covers the vast preponderance of mediations in the literature, but we hope that after several extensions are explicated in this book, we should see more sophisticated analyses and theorizing in the literature).

In the commands that follow, the first line begins with the keyword "Title" and ends in a period. The second line specifies the structure of the data ("da"). This example indicates that the number of input variables ("ni") is three, the number of observations ("no") or sample size is 100, and the matrix ("ma") to be analyzed is the covariance matrix ("cm"). The keyword "la" indicates that the variable labels follow on the next line. The keyword "cm" signals that the covariance matrix is being input in symmetric ("sy") form. The "se" allows the user to select a subset of variables, or reorder the variables because the endogenous variables (i.e., M and Y in a three-variable mediation) must come first.

The model statement ("mo") implies this job is a path model without multiple measures because the number of Y or endogenous variables, 2 (specifically M and Y), is the same as the number of endogenous (eta, η) constructs; similarly, there is a correspondence for X and the exogenous (ksi, ξ) constructs. The factor matrices, lx and ly, are set fixed ("fi") to the identity matrices (again, confirming a one-to-one mapping of the indicator and latent variables), and for the same reason, the measurement error matrices, td and te are fixed to zero. The eta, ksi, lx, ly, td, te matrices are described in greater detail shortly—they will make more sense when we consider multiple variables as indicators of the basic mediation constructs.

The beta (B) and gamma (Γ) matrices are specified by the patterns ("pa"), regarding which paths should be estimated (the "1"s) and which should be fixed to zero (the "0"s). Both the gamma and beta matrices are read such that a column variable is posited to be affecting the row variable. Thus, the single "1" in the beta matrix, $\beta_{2,1}$, indicates that the first endogenous variable (M, according to the "se" listing) has an effect on the second endogenous variable (Y). The outputs are requested via the "ou" command. Readers are encouraged to try the syntax, to test whether they can replicate the findings presented earlier, namely, $a = 0.55$, $b = 0.55$, and $c = 0.15$.

Title: Mediation With Three Constructs, One Measure Each.
da ni=3 no=100 ma=cm
la
x m y
cm sy
1.00
0.55 1.00
0.45 0.63 1.00
se
m y x
mo ny=2 ne=2 nx=1 nk=1 lx=id,fi td=ze,fi ly=id,fi te=ze,fi be=fu,fr ga=fu,fr
pa ga
1
1
pa be
0 0
1 0
out me=ml rs ef

3.4.2   How to Fit Mediation via SEM When Multiple Measures Exist by Incorporating the Measurement Model

Researchers know that reliability is enhanced in the presence of multi-item scales, for X, M, and/or Y, which in turn helps clarify the nature of the relationships among the constructs that the items represent.[7] When working with multi-item scales (e.g., X_1, X_2, X_3 for the independent variable construct, X), it is unclear how to apply the regression-based mediation tests (e.g., imputing X_1, X_2, X_3 into Equations 2.1 to 2.3 would create confusion due to multicollinearity).

Usually, researchers with multi-item scales compute means, resulting in $\overline{X}$, $\overline{M}$, and $\overline{Y}$, which are then imputed into the analogous form of Equations 2.1 to 2.3, namely, Equations 3.15 to 3.17. However, while taking means over multiple items (e.g., $\{X_1, X_2, X_3\} \rightarrow \overline{X}$) to simplify analyses is commonplace, doing so does not use the data to their full advantage as would allowing the representation of the items in a measurement model while fitting the mediation structural model in a structural equations model. When multiple items for X, M, and Y are aggregated to means and analyzed, and the results compared with the use of a full structural equations model (i.e., the inclusion of both the measurement and the path models), perhaps not surprisingly, the latter dominates (Iacobucci et al., 2007). In particular, the full structural equations model properly identifies the population qualities, recovering the proportion of the variance due to the mediated relationship nearly perfectly, whereas the analysis of the means overestimates the extent of mediation (e.g., is biased in favor of concluding partial or full mediation in a sample even in the presence of "none" or "partial" mediation in the population).

Thus, when the researcher has multi-item scales for X, M, or Y, averaging the scales, rather than modeling them via SEM, does a disservice to the data. Within SEM, it is important to let the data speak according to their inherent properties—if there are three indicators of a construct, a properly isomorphic measurement model should be incorporated simultaneously with the structural model seeking to test the mediation rather than collapsing the data to means. Computing means on scales might seem to simplify matters, but simplification in procedural and analytical matters comes at the cost of inaccuracy in substantive and theoretical conclusions—researchers will pay the price for taking this shortcut by often coming to incorrect conclusions about the mediation being tested.

It is not just a "theoretical" argument that the data should be modeled in a manner that represents their structure. It also helps the researcher. When multiple items are modeled in a structural equations model, the measurement error is separated out from the modeling error. Hence, the relationships among the constructs are clarified and usually strengthened. Accordingly, instead of aggregating multi-item scales to means, researchers should run a full structural equations model. The full structural equations model is composed of both the structural model, which specifies the nature of the interrelations among the X, M, and Y constructs, as well as the measurement models, which specify the nature of the mapping from the constructs to their respective indicator variables.

By "multiple" items, we mean scales of length three or more items. In theory, "multi-" item also describes two item scales, but having scales of length three or more helps researchers avoid underidentification (theoretically and empirically unless two or more of the items are extremely highly correlated). Bagozzi and Baumgartner (1994) suggest that scales of length three to five items might be optimal (i.e., three is minimal, more than five may be overkill).

With multi-item scales, in LISREL-notation, we now distinguish ξ, used to denote the *constructs* for the exogenous variables, from the measured exogenous *variables*, the X's. Similarly, η denotes the endogenous constructs, represented by the M's and Y's variables. The full structural equations model is captured by both a structural model

$$\eta = \Gamma \xi + B \eta + \Psi \qquad [3.21]$$

and measurement models, representing the mapping of ξs onto Xs and ηs onto the Ms and Ys:

$$Y = \Lambda_Y \eta + \theta_\varepsilon, \qquad [3.22]$$

$$X = \Lambda_X \xi + \theta_\delta. \qquad [3.23]$$

Consider the scenario of three X variables, three M mediators, and two dependent variables, Y (cf. Equations 3.4 through 3.14). The SEM matrices in Equations 3.21 to 3.23 follow. The structural parameters that are the most theoretically interesting and relevant to the mediation inquiry are Γ and B. Because they are representing three focal constructs, their structure is analogous to the previous scenario (of the path model in which there were only three measures):

$$\Gamma = \begin{matrix} \eta_M \\ \eta_Y \end{matrix} \begin{bmatrix} \gamma_{MX} \\ \gamma_{YX} \end{bmatrix}, \quad B = \begin{matrix} \eta_M \\ \eta_Y \end{matrix} \begin{bmatrix} \beta_{MM}=0 & \beta_{MY}=0 \\ \beta_{YM} & \beta_{YY}=0 \end{bmatrix}.$$

The new matrices in Equations 3.22 and 3.23 include factor loadings for the X and Y variables, contained in the matrices Λ_X and Λ_Y. (Per standard practice, the first loading per factor is fixed to one for standardization purposes.)

$$
\Lambda_X = \begin{array}{c} X_1 \\ X_2 \\ X_3 \end{array}
\overset{\xi}{\begin{bmatrix} \lambda_{X_{11}} = 1 \\ \lambda_{X_{21}} \\ \lambda_{X_{31}} \end{bmatrix}}, \quad
\Lambda_Y = \begin{array}{c} M_1 \\ M_2 \\ M_3 \\ Y_1 \\ Y_2 \end{array}
\overset{\eta_M \qquad \eta_Y}{\begin{bmatrix} \lambda_{Y_{11}} = 1 & 0 \\ \lambda_{Y_{21}} & 0 \\ \lambda_{Y_{31}} & 0 \\ 0 & \lambda_{Y_{42}} = 1 \\ 0 & \lambda_{Y_{52}} \end{bmatrix}}.
$$

Their counterparts, the matrices containing the measurement errors, are Θ_δ and Θ_ε. (Corresponding to the factor loadings that were fixed at 1.0, the corresponding error terms are set to zero in their respective Θ matrices, while the others are estimated.)

$$
\Theta_\delta = \begin{array}{c} X_1 \\ X_2 \\ X_3 \end{array}
\overset{X_1 \quad X_2 \quad X_3}{\begin{bmatrix} \theta_{\delta_{11}} = 0 & 0 & 0 \\ 0 & \theta_{\delta_2} & 0 \\ 0 & 0 & \theta_{\delta_3} \end{bmatrix}}, \quad
\Theta_\varepsilon = \begin{array}{c} M_1 \\ M_2 \\ M_3 \\ Y_1 \\ Y_2 \end{array}
\overset{M_1 \quad M_2 \quad M_3 \quad Y_1 \quad Y_2}{\begin{bmatrix} \theta_{\varepsilon_1} = 0 & 0 & 0 & 0 & 0 \\ 0 & \theta_{\varepsilon_2} & 0 & 0 & 0 \\ 0 & 0 & \theta_{\varepsilon_3} & 0 & 0 \\ 0 & 0 & 0 & \theta_{\varepsilon_4} = 0 & 0 \\ 0 & 0 & 0 & 0 & \theta_{\varepsilon_5} \end{bmatrix}}.
$$

As before, the Ψ matrix contains the endogenous models' lack of fit, analogous to $1 - R^2$. And Φ scales the exogenous construct (and, when there are more than one, captures their intercorrelations):[8]

$$
\Psi = \begin{array}{c} \eta_M \\ \eta_Y \end{array}
\overset{\eta_M \qquad \eta_Y}{\begin{bmatrix} \psi_{\eta_M} & 0 \\ 0 & \psi_{\eta_Y} \end{bmatrix}}, \quad
\Phi = \begin{array}{c} \xi \end{array}
\overset{\xi}{\begin{bmatrix} \phi \end{bmatrix}}.
$$

3.4.3 The LISREL Syntax

The LISREL syntax follows for the model with three constructs, three measures for X, three for M, and two for Y.

Title: Mediation With Three Constructs, 3 X's, 3 M's, and 2 Y's.
da ni=8 no=100 ma=cm
la
x1 x2 x3 m1 m2 m3 y1 y2
cm sy
1.00
0.30 1.00
0.30 0.30 1.00
0.30 0.30 0.30 1.00
0.30 0.30 0.30 0.30 1.00
0.30 0.30 0.30 0.30 0.30 1.00
0.30 0.30 0.30 0.30 0.30 0.30 1.00
0.30 0.30 0.30 0.30 0.30 0.30 0.30 1.00
se
m1 m2 m3 y1 y2 x1 x2 x3
mo ny=5 ne=2 nx=3 nk=1 lx=fu,fr td=di,fr ly=fu,fr te=di,fr be=fu,fr ga=fu,fr
pa lx
0
1
1
pa ly
0 0
1 0
1 0
0 0
0 1
pa ga
1
1
pa be
0 0
1 0
va 1.0 lx(1,1) ly(1,1) ly(4,2)
fi td(1) te(1) te(4)
va 0.0 td(1) te(1) te(4)
out me=ml rs ef

Notes

1. Baron and Kenny (1986) state,

> Generally the effect of measurement error is to attenuate the size of measures of association, the resulting estimate being closer to zero than it would be if there were no measurement error. [For example], measurement error in the mediator [only] is likely to result in an overestimate in the [direct] effect of the independent variable on the dependent variable. (p. 1177)

Bracketed words were inserted for clarification, for example, in contrast, if X and Y were measured with error but M were not, then the mediated path could loom larger than the direct path.

2. Baron and Kenny (1986) continue, "The common approach to unreliability is to have multiple operations or indicators of the construct. . . . One can use the multiple indicator approach and estimate mediation paths by latent-variable structural modeling methods" (p. 1177). Also see http://davidakenny.net/cm/mediate.htm.

3. This result might make researchers deceptively confident that the regression approach is at least "conservative." However, subsequent results show that the regression results are misleading, and the SEM results are closer to the true population parameters (Iacobucci, Saldanha, & Deng, 2007).

4. These studies were important because traditionally it is believed that SEM requires large samples to run well (e.g., $n > 200$). The default computational method in SEM, and the method that is used most often, is maximum likelihood, which produces test statistics that are interpretable asymptotically (i.e., as n increases, the interpretation of the resulting X^2 is more certain), so the question is how large must n be in practice to achieve such stable results. In addition, small samples can cause problems in (non)convergence, for analogous reasons that running regressions with small samples and a large number of predictors creates noisy results. This research suggested that n need not be as high as 200, rather $n = 30$ sufficed. To be fair, the models tested were not terribly complex, but they certainly covered the mediation realm.

5. The first subscript depicts the row of the matrix in which the parameter resides, and the second subscript depicts the column. Hence, γ_{MX} represents the M row and X column of the Γ matrix. Furthermore, the column variable/construct has the impact on the row variable/construct, hence, γ_{MX} represents the effect of $X \rightarrow M$.

6. LISREL is the granddaddy of the packages, and the software syntax is closely linked to the notation. Even most users of other SEM packages usually have some fundamental working knowledge of LISREL and the translation from and to LISREL and their favorite package.

7. Under typical research conditions, researchers diligently try to create a scale that reflects the construct, and the inter-item correlations will be moderate to large. However, even for "bad" scales, with low to moderate inter-item correlations, adding items increases alpha, the typical measure of reliability

Scales can also be multidimensional with relatively high inter-item correlations, thus yielding high alphas, but the ideal for parsimony and definitions of internal consistency is the unidimensional scale—items intended to represent a single construct.

8. With this fuller model depiction, perhaps the simpler three-variable mediation model shown previously is clearer. Specifically, when each of the three constructs is measured by only a single variable, per Equation 3.20, the measurement mapping simplifies to $\Lambda_x = I$, $\Lambda_y = I$,, $\Theta_\delta = 0$, and $\Theta_\varepsilon = 0$ (essentially making the assumption that each construct is being measured without error via its manifest indicator variable). These assumptions, made in most reported mediations, effectively simplify the grander structural equations model to a so-called path model, which contains only the structural model (and no measurement models). In terms of the Equations 3.22 and 3.23, for the three-variable mediation model, $Y = I\eta + 0 = \eta$, $X = I\xi + 0 = \xi$, so the full model 3.21 simplifies from $\eta = \Gamma\xi + B\eta + \Psi$ to $Y = \Gamma X + BY + \Psi$.

CHAPTER 4. MEDIATION WITH STRUCTURAL EQUATIONS MODELING: THE STRUCTURAL MODEL

Structural equations models are composed of a measurement model component and a structural model component. The previous chapter focused on the measurement model. This chapter focuses on the structural model.

Researchers seeking to investigate mediation among the X, M, and Y constructs usually investigate these constructs with a relatively narrow lens that includes only those constructs (e.g., for purposes of efficiency, such as shorter experiments or surveys). However, even if the broader network is not explicitly acknowledged, all construct relationships are implicitly embedded in a larger picture, such as that in Figure 4.1. This broader nomological network is encouraged by philosophers of science and methodologists to offer the richest view of the phenomena and their explanations (Cronbach & Meehl, 1955). For example, in the mediation context, some researchers may wish to examine mediation chains longer than the usual, for example, perhaps $X \to M_1 \to M_2 \to Y$. Other researchers may inquire which of two intervening systems seems to drive the effect of the dependent variable most strongly, for example, in comparing the paths $X \to M_1 \to Y$ and $X \to M_2 \to Y$.

Clearly, the options are nearly endless. Fortunately, in addition to allowing for the incorporation of multi-item measures, SEM easily accommodates the extension of the theorizing beyond the three focal constructs, X, M, and Y. Numerous varieties of broader nomological networks can be modeled, any of which could include constructs depicting additional antecedents or consequences of the focal triad. In this section, we examine the issues that arise, and some that are resolved, with the inclusion of additional constructs.

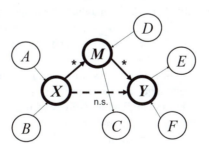

Figure 4.1   Testing Mediation in the Context of a Broader Nomological Network

NOTE. * significant, n.s. = not significant.

4.1 Conceptual Overview

In particular, the addition of at least one more construct, Q, is necessary for state-of-the-art mediation modeling, even if the researcher cares more about X, M, and Y than Q (Bentler, 2001). The primary *theoretical* purpose of the additional construct is the enhanced sophistication of the nomological network, which makes the positing of plausible alternative theories for observed data patterns more difficult to generate, thereby making the nature of the results more statistically and conceptually certain.

The principal *statistical* purpose of the additional construct is to facilitate degrees of freedom. The mediation model posits three links among three constructs so it is characterized as "just identified." One implication of this status is that the directionality of the effects, for example, $X \rightarrow M$ versus $M \rightarrow X$ is empirically indeterminate (MacCallum et al., 1993; McDonald, 2002; also see Fienberg, 1981, pp. 122–123). In the example described previously (wherein $r_{XM} = 0.55$, $r_{XY} = 0.45$, $r_{MY} = 0.63$), the mediation of $X \rightarrow M \rightarrow Y$ yields path coefficients $a = 0.55$, $b = 0.55$, and $c = 0.15$. If the entire directionality were reversed, from $Y \rightarrow M \rightarrow X$, the estimates would be apportioned somewhat differently: 0.63 ($Y \rightarrow M$), 0.44 ($M \rightarrow X$), and 0.17 ($Y \rightarrow X$). If one posited $X \rightarrow Y \rightarrow M$, the estimates would be 0.45 ($X \rightarrow Y$), 0.48 ($Y \rightarrow M$), and 0.33 ($X \rightarrow M$). More problematic is the fact that for all three models (and many more), the fit statistics are indistinguishable and perfect (e.g., Bentler's comparative fit index CFI = 1.00; root mean square error, $RMSE = 0.00$).[1]

Theory should help differentiate alternative models (on the basis of the parameter estimates, which may vary, and not on the basis of the overall fit statistics, which will not); yet competing models are rarely mentioned in the literature and much less frequently tested. Furthermore, rival causal models can be equally plausible from a theoretical perspective. For example, if X = affect, M = cognition, and Y = behavior, there exist supporters of theories that pose $X \rightarrow M$ or $M \rightarrow X$, $M \rightarrow Y$ or $Y \rightarrow M$, and so on (Breckler, 1990).

The use of multi-item scales offers no solution to this problem. It is true that the source covariance matrix is larger, so there appear to be more degrees of freedom, but the additional degrees of freedom are "illusory," in that they contribute to the measurement model accuracy but they do not contribute degrees of freedom to the critical structural model. No matter how many items are measured, with three constructs, there are three inter-construct correlations, and if we seek three path estimates per the mediation analysis, the model is "just identified." However, with four constructs, there are six correlations. If four paths are estimated, 2 spare degrees of

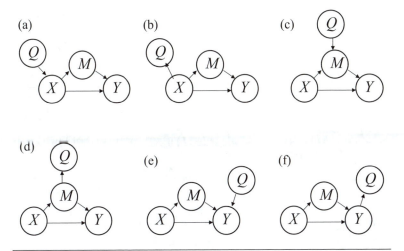

Figure 4.2   All Possible Combinations of Introducing One New Construct via One Path into the Mediation Nomological Network: Q as a Unique Antecedent and Consequence of X, M, and Y

freedom are available to test the superiority of competitive model fits. This scenario of "overdetermination" is preferred because there are fewer unknowns than equations or corresponding data points in the system, so each estimate may be obtained with more certainty.

Figure 4.2 presents all possible positions for a single path involving a single new construct Q, as an antecedent or consequence relating to X, M, and Y, in turn. Naturally, in normal investigations, theory would dictate Q's position, but we examine Q's different roles to make several points about structural equations models and mediations. Each of these recursive, identified, structural models achieves the goal of introducing degrees of freedom for assessing model fit; that is, none of the models is artifactually perfectly fit. However, we shall illustrate that the six models are not equivalent and, in particular, models c and e should not be used.

4.2   Illustration

Let's begin with the running example of $r_{XM} = 0.55$, $r_{XY} = 0.45$, $r_{MY} = 0.63$, which yields path coefficients of $a = 0.55$, $b = 0.55$, $c = 0.15$. These estimates are presented in the upper right of Figure 4.3, for "the baseline model." Let

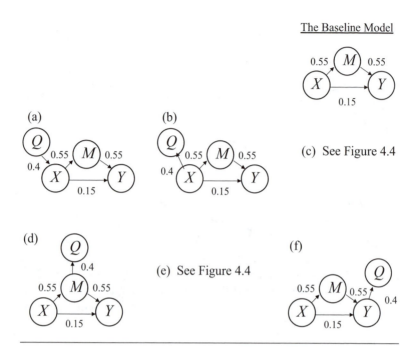

Figure 4.3   The Effect of Q on the X, M, and Y Mediation

us now supplement these correlations by introducing a fourth construct Q. For purposes of illustration, let $r_{QX} = r_{QM} = r_{QY} = 0.40$. In models a, b, d, and f, the three focal path coefficient estimates remain unchanged, and the links involving Q faithfully yield the input relation of 0.40.

Models c and e are presented in Figure 4.4. These models behave differently because the introduction of Q as an antecedent to M or Y means there will be two exogenous constructs (X and Q), which in turn brings a statistical (conceptual and empirical) requirement that their correlation be represented and estimated. Thus, first, while models a, b, d, and f (of Figure 4.3) carry 2 degrees of freedom, models c and e (of Figure 4.4) yield only one (one degree of freedom is used in the estimation of the exogenous intercorrelation).

More problematic is the fact that the three focal mediation path coefficients are no longer invariant. In model c, when Q is a predictor of M (along with X), the resulting multicollinearity between Q and X yields estimates that share the predictive variance, hence, the $Q \rightarrow M$ path is not 0.40 as input, but also the $X \rightarrow M$ path is no longer the 0.55 value we've come

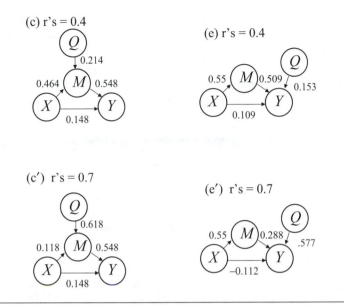

Figure 4.4   Do Not Introduce Q as an Antecedent to M or Y

to expect (as representing the known population structure). Note that the paths involving the prediction of Y (i.e., $M \to Y$ and $X \to Y$) are unaffected. Conversely, in model e, when Q is a predictor of Y (along with X and M), the resulting multicollinearity among X, M, and Y affects each of the paths involving Y: $Q \to Y$ (which we don't care about), and $X \to Y$ and $M \to Y$ (which we do).

For illustration purposes, models c′ and e′ show how the results are affected when the 0.4's (correlations between Q and X, M, and Y) are replaced with 0.7's. The increased multicollinearity creates even more different results (including a sign reversal, indicative of suppressor relationships to compensate for the new highly collinear relationships).

In a sense, the results for these models are certainly "true"; that is, when Q is correlated with X, M, and Y at any level (greater in magnitude than 0.0), the path estimates are those reported. But if the researcher's lens is primarily focused on X, M, and Y, it is best to select a role for Q that does not disturb the central relationships; that is, introduce Q into the model as an antecedent to X or a consequence of X, M, or Y.[2]

These results generalize to the case where the central r_{XM}, r_{XY}, r_{MY} indices vary, that is, regardless of the strength of mediation in the data (e.g., 25% mediated vs. 50% vs. 75%). Second, these results hold as the added r_{QM}, r_{QX}, r_{QY} relationships are stronger, weaker, or vary (e.g., as the 0.40 and 0.70 contrast demonstrates).

To get a sense of what is going on, a simple way to think of the essence of mediation is that the partial correlation between X and Y would be zero when statistically controlling for their relationships with M:

$$r_{XY \bullet M} = \frac{r_{XY} - r_{XM} r_{YM}}{\sqrt{\left(1 - r_{XM}^2\right)\left(1 - r_{YM}^2\right)}}$$

(James & Brett, 1984); in words, "The complete mediation model thus predicts that X has a direct effect on M, M has a direct effect on Y, and X is not related directly to Y when M is held constant." Recall our caution that this partial correlation is consistent with the $X \to M \to Y$ mediation supposition, but also with the reverse causal chain, $Y \to M \to X$ or the positing of M as a common factor giving rise to X and Y, that is, $X \leftarrow M \to Y$ (McDonald, 2001). In SEM, the equivalency in these relationships translates into the fact that without Q, the omnibus fit statistics for these models will be identical: All goodness-of-fit measures (e.g., R^2s) will equal one; all badness-of-fit measures (e.g., χ^2; SRMR and other indices based on residuals) will equal zero.[3] However, one starting point would be to fit the desired mediation model, per Figure 1.1, and then proceed to fit alternative competing models, beginning with $Y \to M \to X$, but also including other roles for the mediator construct, say $M \to X \to Y$, or $X \to Y \to M$, and show that while the overall fit statistics might be the same, the appropriate parameter estimates are not significant, or the parameter estimates are nonsensical on theoretical grounds.

With the inclusion of Q, the additional degrees of freedom allow us to compare model fits, though to be fair, with only 2 degrees of freedom, first, the model fits are likely to be somewhat comparable, and second, excessive Type I errors can result from comparing too many competing models. For the classic mediation model, $X \to M \to Y$, and $Q \to X$ the basic fits are GFI = 0.96; RMR = 0.09; CFI = 0.96. When the entire direction of causality is reversed, $Y \to M \to X$ (and $Q \to X$), the model fits are as follows: GFI = 0.91; RMR = 0.20; CFI = 0.86. When the pattern is tested $M \to X \to Y$, the fits are GFI = 0.98; RMR = 0.038; CFI = 0.99. These batteries of indices suggest a slight advantage to the last model, though as anticipated.

Without the additional construct, the central three-construct model is "just identified," another way of saying that many competing models will fit equally well. Problems of identification and alternative models in SEM are discussed at length in MacCallum et al. (1993). Even without the problem of statistically identical models, strong theory is essential to the researcher hoping to make progress in arguing for, or against, mediations. Consider the following:

> A well-fitting model is one that closely reproduces the observed data. However, even when a model is found to be consistent with the data, it is almost always the case that alternative models will be equally consistent. . . . Stelzl (1986) has developed several rules that help to generate a family of equivalent models. . . . Two equivalent models will account for the same observed covariances equally well; every global goodness of fit statistic will be identical for the two models. . . . However, two equivalent models can differ in the values estimated for individual parameters, thereby providing some basis for distinguishing between them. (Breckler 1990, p. 262)

Given the importance of the caution of overinterpreting correlational data as evidence for mediation (or other causal structures), and the importance of theory to supplement empirical results, we offer two more illustrations. First, imagine two fully mediated scenarios, one in which the mediator is closer conceptually or temporally to X, perhaps M is measured so closely in time or modality that method variance might further connect the X and M variables. This closeness might be depicted as $X \to M \longrightarrow Y$, and empirically might be represented by say, $r_{XM} = 0.90$, $r_{XY} = 0.30$, and $r_{MY} = 0.30$. We can contrast that scenario with one in which the mediator is more highly correlated with Y, depicted as $X \longrightarrow M \to Y$, say, with $r_{XM} = 0.30$, $r_{XY} = 0.30$, and $r_{MY} = 0.90$. If we fit the mediation model to each data set, in the first scenario, the path coefficient estimates are $\gamma_{MX} = 0.90$ ($p < .05$), $\gamma_{YX} = 0.15$ ($p > .05$), and $\beta_{YM} = 0.15$ ($p > .05$) (for a percentage mediation of 47.4%); in the second, the estimates are $\gamma_{MX} = 0.30$ ($p < .05$), $\gamma_{YX} = 0.03$ ($p > .05$), and $\beta_{YM} = 0.89$ ($p < .05$) (resulting in a percentage mediation of 89.9%). The significance and insignificance of these parameter estimates indicate that mediation would be supported for the second scenario, but not the first, although conceptually both appear to be mediation chains.[4]

4.3 Suppression

The second illustration involves suppression, an issue discussed in the mediation literature. MacKinnon, Krull, and Lockwood (2000) compare the effects of mediation and suppression:

> In [mediation] . . . , it is typically assumed that . . . the relationship between the independent and dependent variables . . . is reduced because the mediator explains part or all of the relationship. . . . However, it is possible that the

... removal of a [variable] could increase the magnitude of the relationship between the independent and dependent variable. Such a change would indicate suppression. (p. 174)

They offer an example: Imagine X is a measure of employee intelligence; M, a measure of their boredom; and Y, the number of errors made on an assembly line job. A human resources researcher would expect to see $r_{XM} > 0$, $r_{MY} > 0$, yet r_{XY} would likely be negative.

A diagnostic of suppression specifically in the mediation (and SEM) framework would be that the sign of $a \times b$ (i.e., $\gamma_{MX} \times \beta_{YM}$) is the opposite of the sign of c (i.e., γ_{YX}; MacKinnon et al., 2000, p. 174; Shrout & Bolger, 2002, p. 432; Tzelgov & Henik, 1991). Suppression is something that most social scientists have heard of, but are not terribly familiar with, so another example may be useful. Shrout and Bolger (2002, p. 431) offer the following. Suppose X is a stressor of some sort; M, a coping behavior (e.g., support seeking); and Y, the level of distress experienced. A clinician would expect to see $r_{XM} > 0$ and $r_{MY} < 0$, so the mediated, indirect path would be negative. Finally, r_{XY} would likely be positive; hence the signs of the $a \times b$ product (for the mediated path) and c (the direct path) would be opposite, indicative of suppression.

Another way to think about suppression is to contrast it with multicollinearity. With multicollinearity, we can see "examples where a predictor has a strong effect by itself on the outcome but a negligible effect after adjusting for another predictor" where in contrast, suppression is "the opposite condition where a predictor has a negligible effect by itself yet takes on a stronger effect after adjusting for another predictor" (Lynn, 2003, p. 58). For example, let Y be a dependent variable, A be a predictor variable, and B be another predictor that is correlated with A ($r_{AB} \neq 0$), uncorrelated with Y ($r_{BY} = 0$), causing the R^2 (for the multiple regression predicting Y using both A and B as predictors) to exceed the sum of the two squared simple correlations (i.e., $R^2 > (r_{AY}^2 + r_{BY}^2)$)—$B$ is said to be a suppressor variable.

The point of these examples is to remind potential mediation modelers that the perpetual saying, "garbage in, garbage out" is applicable here too. Without strong, clear theorizing, including the willingness to test competing theories, the statistical machinery of mediation analyses cannot magically clarify data structures.

In the sections that follow, we close this chapter with the LISREL syntax for the scenarios we have been presenting with more constructs than the three focal mediation constructs. In the next chapter, we turn to data analysis scenarios that are more complicated yet.

4.4 LISREL Syntax for Four-Construct Models

In this section, the LISREL syntax is offered for each of the four recommended models in Figure 4.3. In this first syntax, Q serves as an antecedent to X:

Title: Four Constructs, Q→X (Figure 4.3a).
da ni=4 no=100 ma=cm
la
x m y q
cm sy
1.00
0.30 1.00
0.30 0.30 1.00
0.30 0.30 0.30 1.00
mo ny=3 ne=3 nx=1 nk=1 lx=id,fi td=ze,fi ly=id,fi te=ze,fi be=fu,fr ga=fu,fr
pa ga
1
0
0
pa be
0 0 0
1 0 0
1 1 0
out me=ml rs ef

In this second input listing, Q is a consequence of X:

Title: Four Constructs, Q→X (Figure 4.3b).
da ni=4 no=100 ma=cm
la
x m y q
cm sy
1.00
0.30 1.00
0.30 0.30 1.00
0.30 0.30 0.30 1.00
mo ny=3 ne=3 nx=1 nk=1 lx=id,fi td=ze,fi ly=id,fi te=ze,fi be=fu,fr ga=fu,fr
pa ga
1
0
0

42

```
pa be
0 0 0
1 0 0
1 1 0
out me=ml rs ef
```

In this third model, *Q* is a consequence of *M:*

```
Title: Four Constructs, M→Q (Figure 4.3d).
da ni=4 no=100 ma=cm
la
x m y q
cm sy
1.00
0.30 1.00
0.30 0.30 1.00
0.30 0.30 0.30 1.00
se
m y q x
mo ny=3 ne=3 nx=1 nk=1 lx=id,fi td=ze,fi ly=id,fi te=ze,fi be=fu,fr ga=fu,fr
pa ga
1
1
0
pa be
0 0 0
1 0 0
1 0 0
out me=ml rs ef
```

In this fourth and final model, *Q* is a consequence of *Y:*

```
Title: Four Constructs, Y→Q (Figure 4.3f).
da ni=4 no=100 ma=cm
la
x m y q
cm sy
1.00
0.30 1.00
0.30 0.30 1.00
0.30 0.30 0.30 1.00
```

```
se
m y q x
mo ny=3 ne=3 nx=1 nk=1 lx=id,fi td=ze,fi ly=id,fi te=ze,fi be=fu,fr ga=fu,fr
pa ga
1
1
0
pa be
0 0 0
1 0 0
0 1 0
out me=ml rs ef
```

4.5   LISREL Syntax for a Longer Mediation Chain and Alternative Mediation Paths

This syntax is offered for the prototype case where a fourth construct lengthens the mediation chain, $X \rightarrow M_1 \rightarrow M_2 \rightarrow Y$:

```
Title: X to M1 to M2 to Y.
da ni=4 no=100 ma=cm
la
x m1 m2 y
cm sy
1.00
0.30 1.00
0.30 0.30 1.00
0.30 0.30 0.30 1.00
se
m1 m2 y x
mo ny=3 ne=3 nx=1 nk=1 lx=id,fi td=ze,fi ly=id,fi te=ze,fi be=fu,fr ga=fu,fr
pa ga
1
0
1
pa be
0 0 0
1 0 0
0 1 0
out me=ml rs ef
```

This syntax examines two branching mediation paths, $X \to M_1 \to Y$ and $X \to M_2 \to Y$:

```
Title: X through M1 to Y and X through M2 to Y.
da ni=4 no=100 ma=cm
la
x m1 m2 y
cm sy
1.00
0.30 1.00
0.30 0.30 1.00
0.30 0.30 0.30 1.00
se
m1 m2 y x
mo ny=3 ne=3 nx=1 nk=1 lx=id,fi td=ze,fi ly=id,fi te=ze,fi be=fu,fr ga=fu,fr
pa ga
1
1
1
pa be
0 0 0
0 0 0
1 1 0
out me=ml rs ef
```

This LISREL syntax shows how to test for mediation in the context of a larger, much more complex nomological network, specifically the structure depicted in Figure 4.1.

```
Title: Nine Constructs, per Figure 4.1.
da ni=9 no=100 ma=cm
la
x m y a b c d e f
cm sy
1.00
0.30 1.00
0.30 0.30 1.00
0.30 0.30 0.30 1.00
0.30 0.30 0.30 0.30 1.00
0.30 0.30 0.30 0.30 0.30 1.00
0.30 0.30 0.30 0.30 0.30 0.30 1.00
0.30 0.30 0.30 0.30 0.30 0.30 0.30 1.00
0.30 0.30 0.30 0.30 0.30 0.30 0.30 0.30 1.00
```

se
x m y c e a b d f
mo ny=5 ne=5 nx=4 nk=4 lx=id,fi td=ze,fi ly=id,fi te=ze,fi be=fu,fr ga=fu,fr
pa ga
1 1 0 0
0 0 1 0
0 0 0 1
0 0 0 0
0 0 0 0
pa be
0 0 0 0 0
1 0 0 0 0
1 1 0 0 0
0 1 0 0 0
0 0 1 0 0
out me=ml rs ef

4.6 Significance of the Indirect Effect

Ultimately, the question of mediation is one of distinguishing the extent
to which the effect of X on Y is direct $(X \to Y)$ or indirect through the
mediator $(X \to M \to Y)$. Structural equations modelers have explored the
estimates and significance tests of this decomposition (cf. Bollen, 1987;
Holbert & Stephenson, 2003; Preacher & Hayes, 2004).

In the simple mediation scheme (e.g., as first presented in Figure 1.1),
the direct effect of X on Y is estimated by coefficient c (or γ_{YX} in the LIS-
REL model), the indirect effect of X on Y via M is estimated by the product
of the relevant structural coefficients ($a \times b$; or $\gamma_{MX} \times \beta_{YM}$ in the LISREL
model), and the total effect of X on Y via direct and indirect paths is their
sum: $[c + (a \times b)]$.

The parsing of total effects into those that are direct and indirect is available via options in most of the SEM software. For example, in LISREL,
the "ef" keyword on the output line produces the direct, indirect, and total
effects estimates.

From the output of the statistical computing packages, the direct, indirect, and total effects may be obtained. The significance of these individual
components may also be obtained. Theoretically, the z test in Equation 2.4
is analogous to the significance test of the indirect effect; specifically, the
results should converge qualitatively (either significant or not), even if the
actual values vary somewhat. Finally, whether the direct or indirect effects

are significant or not, it remains a scientific judgment of the researcher to make conclusive statements regarding the relative size of the impact on Y of the direct and indirect paths.

4.7 Remaining Issues

If the researcher has additional constructs, for example, per Figure 4.1 or 4.3, there are more degrees of freedom to use. When there exist more degrees of freedom, comparative fit statistics can be obtained, that is, the difference in two X^2s (i.e., ΔX^2 like a ΔR^2 in regression) of nested models (e.g., Model 1 with predictors X, M of Y nested in Model 2 with predictors X, M, Q, W of Y via $\Delta X^2 = X_1^2 - X_2^2$ on $\Delta df = df_1 - df_2$).

Fitting hierarchically nested models is not necessary; however, they offer the analyst another vantage. Yet here is the issue: Whether fit via the old-fashioned regressions or the more appropriate contemporary structural equations models, the mediation questions will almost always certainly be examined in data sets containing multicollinearity among predictors. Consider that one of the conditions to conclude the existence of mediation is that X is related to M; that is, $X \rightarrow M$ (the first half of the mediation path). Accordingly, when focusing on the prediction and explanation of Y, the direct path (comprising X) and the indirect path (comprising X and M) is estimated via two predictors that are themselves correlated—the definition of multicollinearity.

Multicollinearity affects the estimation, significance tests of, and therefore interpretation of structural path coefficients βs and γs in structural equations models (or βs in regression), but the overall fit indices are not affected (X^2 or R^2). Multicollinearity affects the apportioning of the variance attributable to the different predictors, but not the overall assessment of how much variance is explained by their collectivity. Thus, researchers concerned with multicollinearity may not wish to study the structural path parameter estimates, and instead study the overall fits and their comparative indices for nested models. Unfortunately, the idea of fitting nested models reverts the path modeling procedures to more sophisticated versions of the original regression modeling procedure of fitting multiple models, which was criticized as creating a testing context in which models of apples were compared with models of oranges.

Treatments and concern regarding multicollinearity border on the philosophical, and another view defends the examination of the β and γ estimates because data of any interest will naturally demonstrate some multicollinearity. Fitting one simultaneous model, with the direct link

$(X \rightarrow Y)$ and the indirect link $(X \rightarrow M \rightarrow Y)$, as well as any other links among any other constructs, may indeed include multicollinearity, but the idea of the simultaneous fitting is that all effects are estimated while partialling out, or statistically controlling for, the other effects in the model.

Notes

1. It is the "just identified" modeling problem (zero degrees of freedom, spuriously perfect fits, etc.) that led some researchers to advocate that while structural equations models should be used, the researcher should fit two models (one with the $X \rightarrow M \rightarrow Y$ paths, which would use only 2 df (leaving one remaining to assess fit), and one model (say with only the direct path, $X \rightarrow Y$ for comparison, or all three paths, to assess potential partial mediation). Unfortunately, such an approach perpetuates the idea of fitting multiple models, when a single model, with all parameters simultaneously estimated, is statistically superior. Furthermore, while the fits will be identical, different permutations of relationships among the three central constructs can result in different estimates, as we have shown, and some may be more theoretically sensible than others.

2. If one's desired nomological network embeds the X, M, Y focal mediation triangle in a manner such that M or Y have an antecedent, then indeed, the researcher should test that model. Theory supercedes statistics; statistics are a tool for theory testing. Estimation and testing would simply proceed as in regression in the presence of multicollinearity; that is, the interpretation of the parameter estimates must be more tentative, given the sharing of variance across correlated constructs.

3. The model positing a common factor (M) yielding both X and Y is estimated on one degree of freedom; hence, the fits will (typically) be imperfect, and informative, compared with the trivially fitting saturated models.

4. These contrasting scenarios also illustrate the notion that the Sobel (1982) z test, $z = (a \times b) / \sqrt{b^2 s_a^2 + a^2 s_b^2}$, is maximally powerful as a and b approach comparability in size. For example, the numerator product would be $(0.9)(0.15) = 0.135$ in the first scenario, and $(0.3)(0.89) = 0.267$ in the second. If either a or b is small, the product with the other coefficient, even if the other is substantial, will be greatly reduced.

CHAPTER 5. ADVANCED TOPICS

In this chapter, we examine a variety of more complicated data scenarios in which the researcher seeks to understand mediation. First, we apply the SEM to "mediated moderation." In general, "moderation" is interpreted simply as the presence of an interaction to capture a contingent relationship. In mediated moderation, the relationship between an interaction (product) term and the dependent variable is mediated.

Second, we turn to the case of "moderated mediation." In this scenario, the question is whether some variable moderates the mediation or tempers the strength of the mediation. In the simplest, and most common situation, there are two groups, and the research question is whether mediation is occurring in one group but not in another. That is, if there is mediation, $X \rightarrow M \rightarrow Y$ in one group, but a direct relationship in the other, $X \rightarrow Y$, then the group variable is the moderator. The moderator might be more complex (e.g., a continuous variable, not just a distinction between two groups), and we examine that scenario as well.

Third, we examine what the researcher should do whose variables are categorical. Fourth, we explore the issues underlying longitudinal data.

5.1   Mediated Moderation

The inquiry into "mediated moderation" is defined as a mediation model involving an interaction term (Muller, Judd, & Yzerbyt, 2005). When conducting an experiment, a researcher manipulates factors X_1 and X_2, and a classic analysis of variance would model the dependent measure Y as a function of these two main effects, as well as their interaction term, $X_1 * X_2$. Analogously, in the context of mediation analyses, moderation is taken to be represented by an interaction term, nothing more or less.

The mediation question is the same as always, it simply involves a moderating term; that is, is there a direct effect from $\{X_1 * X_2\} \rightarrow Y$, or an indirect, mediated effect, $\{X_1 * X_2\} \rightarrow M \rightarrow Y$.

As depicted in Figure 5.1, the main effects are also included in the model for the purposes of statistical control (to partial out the lower-order terms and their related but extraneous variance and covariance); however, they are not of focal substantive interest. The question of whether the moderator is mediated (i.e., "Is there mediated moderation?") has us focused on assessing the relative size of the indirect path parameter estimate product,

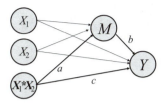

Figure 5.1   Mediated Moderation

$a \times b$ (i.e., $\gamma_{M,X_1 * X_2} \times \beta_{YM}$) versus the direct path c (i.e., $\gamma_{Y,X_1 * X_2}$) parameter estimate.[1]

If theory requires the testing of mediated moderation, then these methods are the means by which such an investigation should be conducted. However, while interaction terms are commonplace, indeed expected, in the analysis of variance for experimental factors, they have been documented as somewhat problematic when operationalized as continuous variables, with the interaction manifest by a product term. Issues that arise in the application of the general linear model with continuous predictors and their product terms apply here also. In particular, researchers should center the main effect variables about their means prior to computing the product term to reduce the resulting multicollinearity among the product and its components, and researchers may wish to examine plots of the data to examine the extent to which the computed term created intractable nonlinearities against which linear models might not be robust (James & Brett, 1984, p. 310), and so on.[2]

Should the predictors be represented by multiple indicators, the means on their respective scales should be multiplied to obtain a single item to represent the interaction term. For example, X_{1a}, X_{1b}, X_{1c} would be combined to $\overline{X}_1$; X_{2a}, X_{2b}, X_{2c} combined to $\overline{X}_2$, and a product term created $\overline{X}_1 \times \overline{X}_2$.

In sum, for mediated moderation, the main effect factors are included in the model essentially to serve as control variables (analogous to the analysis of variance), because the interest is more in how the $X_1 * X_2$ term behaves. Whether the $X_1 \rightarrow M$, $X_1 \rightarrow Y$, $X_2 \rightarrow M$, $X_2 \rightarrow Y$ paths are significant or not is irrelevant. Those estimates are set aside and mediation proceeds with the $X_1 * X_2 \rightarrow M$, $X_1 * X_2 \rightarrow Y$ estimates.

The LISREL syntax to fit the model depicted in Figure 5.1 is as follows:

Title: X1, X2, and X1*X2 each to M and to Y.
da ni=5 no=100 ma=cm
la
x1 x2 x12 m y
cm sy
1.00
0.30 1.00
0.30 0.30 1.00
0.30 0.30 0.30 1.00
0.30 0.30 0.30 0.30 1.00
se
m y x1 x2 x12
mo ny=2 ne=2 nx=3 nk=3 lx=id,fi td=ze,fi ly=id,fi te=ze,fi be=fu,fr ga=fu,fr
pa ga
1 1 1
1 1 1
pa be
0 0
1 0
out me=ml rs ef

Finally, note that there will be sufficient degrees of freedom to estimate this model. There are five constructs, so we will draw from 10 covariances, to estimate seven paths.

5.2   Moderated Mediation

The concept of "moderated mediation" captures the idea that the nature of the mediated relationship is contingent on the levels of some moderator variable: for example, perhaps mediation occurs in one sample but not another, or perhaps mediation is stronger as another variable increases, and so on (cf. Muller et al., 2005).

Typically, the moderator is a categorical variable, and even more frequently, that categorical variable is binary. That is, there are two groups, and researchers are interested in establishing evidence that a mediated relationship exists in one sample but a direct relationship exists in the other. The groups may be defined by experimental conditions or individual differences variables such as gender or median splits on scales measuring traits, and so on. (Less frequently, moderators are continuous, and their treatment will be discussed at the end of this section.)

Testing for moderated mediation would be difficult using the old-fashioned regression approach. Dummy variables depicting group membership and their interactions with the component path coefficients may be used via the regression techniques, but the approach would be clumsy. SEM has a natural methodological counterpart to enable testing of this substantive inquiry. In LISREL and other SEM software, there exist syntax options to fit "multigroup" structural equations models. Per Figure 5.2, the model is specified for each group as having all three paths, but the theoretical prediction is essentially that the direct link, c, is significant in one group, and the indirect path, the a and b estimates, significant in the other.

In the estimation, the first covariance matrix is entered and the model specified with all three (direct and indirect) paths. The second covariance matrix follows in the syntax (to be shown shortly), and the user may specify either that the "pattern" of coefficients is the same in both groups or that the coefficients cross-validate identically (i.e., they are "invariant" across the groups).

If the researcher is working with only the three focal constructs, X, M, and Y, asking that the *same pattern* of relationships be fit in the two samples will result in perfect fits in either sample (due to the aforementioned issue of the models being just identified). The parameter estimates may vary, and these differences may suffice in distinguishing the two groups, establishing mediation in one group and a direct link in another. For example, if we take p_1 to be the proportion of variance in Y in Group 1 explained by the mediation, $p_1 = (a_1 \times b_1 / (a_1 \times b_1) + c_1)$, and p_2 to be the proportion of variance in Y in Group 2 explained by mediation, $p_2 = (a_2 \times b_2 / (a_2 \times b_2) + c_2)$, we can conduct a standard z test to compare the size of these proportions:

$$z = \frac{p_1 - p_2}{\sqrt{\dfrac{p_1(1-p_1)}{n_1} + \dfrac{p_2(1-p_2)}{n_2}}},$$

Group I:
Direct Relationship Hypothesized

Group II:
Mediated Relationship Hypothesized

Figure 5.2 Moderated Mediation

and if this $z > 1.96$, the proportion of mediation is greater in Group 1. If $z < -1.96$, the proportion of mediation is greater in Group 2. If this z is not significant, the strengths of the mediation paths are comparable in the two groups.

Alternatively, with only X, M, and Y, the researcher seeking a nontrivial fit statistic must test the *invariance* option. Here, the parameters are equated, $a = a'$, $b = b'$, and $c = c'$, and the researcher seeking to demonstrate moderated mediation would want statistics that indicate that the model (of such parameter equation) does not fit.

When researchers are working with X, M, Y embedded in the more complex network (i.e., with Q), the invariance model would be estimated, and once again, the fit statistics should indicate that the model does not fit. If the model does not fit, the user should rerun the LISREL job, this time requesting the same "pattern" in estimation to obtain the apparently different parameter estimates, to see which group demonstrates the stronger mediation effect.

The LISREL syntax to fit the basic three-variable mediation in two groups is as follows:

```
Title: Moderated Mediation.
da ng=2 ni=3 no=100 ma=cm
la
x m y
cm sy
1.00
0.30 1.00
0.30 0.30 1.00
se
m y x
mo ny=2 ne=2 nx=1 nk=1 lx=id,fi td=ze,fi ly=id,fi te=ze,fi be=fu,fr ga=fu,fr
pa ga
1
1
pa be
0 0
1 0
out me=ml rs ef
da ni=3 no=100 ma=cm
la
x m y
cm sy
```

```
1.00
0.30 1.00
0.30 0.30 1.00
se
m y x
mo be=ps ga=ps
out me=ml rs ef
```

In the second model ("mo") statement, this syntax example proclaims the "ps" or "same pattern" option (to obtain the likely different parameter estimates). When researchers fit the "invariant" model, the "in" option is used instead.

Consider an example of moderated mediation. A data set was built to exhibit 75% mediation in Group 1 and 25% mediation in Group 2, the fits were marginal ($X_3^2 = 7.05$, $p = .07$; CFI = .97). Hence, we would stop, concluding that no matter the appearance to the eye, the amount of mediation in both groups was essentially statistically equivalent. By comparison, when we tested 100% mediation in Group 1 and 0% in Group 2, the model clearly did not fit ($X_3^2 = 22.01$, $p = .00$; CFI = .57). For this scenario, we know the mediation strengths differ—the lack of fit demonstrates that the structure of relationships in Group 1 was significantly different from that in Group 2.

This treatment of moderated mediation was premised on the moderator being categorical, and whether the categorical variable takes on two or more levels, those two or more groups are easily accommodated via multigroup analyses. However, a question arises as to how to proceed if the moderator is not a discrete variable. We address this issue next.

Say for the moment we were modeling only $X \rightarrow Y$. If we were to pose the question, "Is this relationship moderated?" we would introduce the moderator as a main effect (for statistical control purposes) and as an interaction term, in total introducing two new paths: $Mod \rightarrow Y$ and $\{X * Mod\} \rightarrow Y$.

In the fuller mediation scenario, we proceed analogously. Thus, if the moderator in the moderated mediation is continuous, we introduce terms $Mod \rightarrow Y$ and $\{X * Mod\} \rightarrow Y$, as well as $Mod \rightarrow M$, $\{X * Mod\} \rightarrow M$, and $\{M * Mod\} \rightarrow Y$. The model resembles that in Figure 5.3.

This figure resembles Figure 5.1 somewhat, but the two should not be confused. In Figure 5.1 (mediated moderation), all main effects and interactions are included in the model, but the mediation analysis focuses only on the "usual" three parameters, a, b, and c. In Figure 5.3, there are even more terms, and again, almost all of them are merely serving as statistical

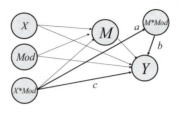

Figure 5.3   Moderated Mediation for a Continuous Moderator

controls. The highlighted paths, *a*, *b*, and *c* are those of focus, but their interpretation is a bit more complicated.

Say the moderator is a measure of extraversion, with higher numbers representing more extraverted respondents. The coefficient *a* will be positive when the $X \rightarrow M$ path is stronger for the extraverts, path *b* will be positive when the $M \rightarrow Y$ path is stronger for extraverts, and path *c* will be positive when the $X \rightarrow Y$ path is stronger for extraverts. The strengths of the path coefficients *a*, *b*, and *c* can still be compared via the *z* test of Equation 2.4.

Clearly, this technique subsumes the modeling of a binary moderator, in which case the analysis should resemble (roughly) that of the multigroup analysis discussed previously. Say the measure of extraversion were converted to a binary variable via a median split, coded 0 = introverted, 1 = extraverted. In this scenario, coefficient *a* is positive if there is an $X \rightarrow M$ path for extraverts, *b* is positive if there is a path from $M \rightarrow Y$ for extraverts, and *c* is positive if there is an $X \rightarrow Y$ path for extraverts. The coding (0/1) can be reversed and the analyses rerun for a complementary perspective to understand the data from the introverts' point of view.

Note that there will be sufficient degrees of freedom to estimate this model. There are six constructs, so the 15 covariances provide enough information to estimate eight paths.

5.3   Categorical Variables

The traditional and SEM approaches for examining mediation structures work well on continuous variables (e.g., even variables measured on 5- or 7-point rating scales). However, increasingly, a number of important variables of central interest in the social sciences are discrete, or categorical in nature (e.g., yes/no). In this section, we illustrate methods for handling categorical variables in mediation studies.

For example, in behavioral decision theory (or judgment and decision making), a researcher might be interested in whether a personality trait such as risk seeking (X) affects the choice to engage in extreme sports (Y) through current life assessment (M), where Y is categorical. Or, a marketing researcher might be interested in whether expertise (X) affects customer satisfaction (Y) through brand choice (M), where M is categorical. Similarly, political ideology may be continuous (X), party affiliation discrete (M), and attitudes toward a Presidential action continuous (Y) (Winship & Mare, 1983).

Sometimes the information is inherently categorical, such as gender or ethnicity. Sometimes continuous information is categorized, for example, transforming household income into three or four classes of socioeconomic status or performing median splits on scales measuring respondent traits, and so on.[3]

In mediation analysis, categorical X variables would not be terribly problematic—the $X \rightarrow M$ and $X \rightarrow Y$ paths could be estimated via dummy variables serving in the structural equations models. What offers a greater challenge, however, would be categorical variables in the role of the mediator, M, or the dependent variable, Y. We first present the problem and then we present solutions.

5.3.1 The Nature of the Categorical Problem

Let us begin with a classic concern that categorized versions of underlying continuous variables suffer a "loss of information," with the result that the strengths of empirical relationships involving the categorized variables are dampened. Table 5.1 contains the results of eight mediation structural equation models. A data set with $n = 10,000$ observations was generated to display 25% mediation.[4] The first row, Model A, treats all three variables, X, M, and Y, in their original continuous form, thus these results essentially form the truth against which we will compare the other treatments of the data.

In the remainder of the table, Models B through H, each of the variables is noted as to whether it is modeled in its original continuous form, or is treated as categorical, made binary via the commonly used mechanism of a median split. The comparisons yield observations that are noteworthy and yet not surprising.

Compare the numbers within the column labeled "a," which represents the parameter estimate on the $X \rightarrow M$ path. When Y, the variable not

TABLE 5.1

Treating Continuous X, M, Y Variables as Binary

Model	X	M	Y	a $X \rightarrow M$	c $X \rightarrow Y$	b $M \rightarrow Y$	$ab/$ $(ab+c)$	R_M^2	R_Y^2
A	Continuous	Continuous	Continuous	0.321	0.298	0.309	0.250	0.103	0.244
B	Continuous	Continuous	Categorical	0.321	0.248	0.249	0.244	0.103	0.163
C	Continuous	Categorical	Continuous	0.252	0.338	0.237	0.150	0.064	0.210
D	Continuous	Categorical	Categorical	0.252	0.276	0.206	0.158	0.064	0.148
E	Categorical	Continuous	Continuous	0.263	0.230	0.345	0.283	0.069	0.214
F	Categorical	Continuous	Categorical	0.263	0.192	0.278	0.276	0.069	0.142
G	Categorical	Categorical	Continuous	0.202	0.267	0.268	0.169	0.041	0.172
H	Categorical	Categorical	Categorical	0.202	0.218	0.232	0.177	0.041	0.122

involved in this path, is treated as categorical (Model B), the $X \rightarrow M$ path coefficient remains unaffected (compared to Model A). When M is treated categorically (Models C and D), or X is treated categorically (Models E and F), the estimate is truncated. The truncation effect is further exaggerated when both M and X are binary (models G and H), compared with their original continuous status. Similar observations can be made in the columns corresponding to the $X \rightarrow Y$ or $M \rightarrow Y$ paths (e.g., compare Model A with Models B, E, and F for $X \rightarrow Y$, or Model A to Models B, C, and D for $M \rightarrow Y$).[5]

Another way to think about "loss of information" is that the variance inherent to a binary variable (whether naturally binary, or naturally continuous and subsequently dichotomized) is reduced (e.g., the extreme would be $\sigma_X^2 = 0$). Thus, it has less potential as a predictor in explaining variance in some dependent variable.

A different kind of observation may also be seen in the mediation models in Table 5.1. Given that there is more than one relationship being compared, when one path is weakened, the overall effect can appear to strengthen another path. For example, in the column labeled "c," the $X \rightarrow Y$ path is estimated as relatively stronger when the mediator M is made categorical (compare Models A and C). The loss of information on M truncates the relationships between M and other variables (specifically $X \rightarrow M$ and $M \rightarrow Y$), effectively highlighting the relationships among the other non-M variables (notably, $X \rightarrow Y$). Similarly, in the third column, the $M \rightarrow Y$ path is heightened when the X variable is categorical (compare Models A and E). These results are "correct," but they should flag a researcher (or reviewer) that the treatment of a variable (or its inherent continuous vs.

categorical status) can clearly affect whether variance seems to be going from X to Y directly or indirectly via M.

For example, a researcher wishing to make the case that the mediation path is weak so that therefore the conceptualization should be considered direct (i.e., that $X \rightarrow Y$ dominates $X \rightarrow M \rightarrow Y$) could achieve an empirical basis for such a statement simply by categorizing the intervening variable, M. Conversely, the researcher entertaining the hypothesis of mediation might set up X to be discrete, as is the case for researchers using experimental manipulations or group memberships as the independent variables. Of course, these treatments of the data would mask the underlying true effects and produce misleading results. Instead, one ethical implication is that the researcher seeking to support evidence of a direct effect might be certain that the mediator is continuous and not discrete, and the researcher hoping to support a mediated path would make sure X was continuous; at the least, these researchers would be setting higher, more conservative hurdles that the mediation statistics must clear.

The intent of this illustration is not to criticize the use of categorical versions of continuous variables—sometimes that information is all that is available to the researcher, sometimes the logical comparisons of a few categorical points is all that is required for the researcher to make a theoretical test, and sometimes the continuous version of a scale is misleading in being seemingly overly precise, and so on. Researchers must work with whatever their form of variables, or whatever form suits their overarching theoretical purposes.[6] This illustration is intended to serve as a caution once again against overly eagerly interpreting correlational data (and data with error due to sampling, measurement error, truncation, etc.) as evidence of a causal chain.

5.3.2 Solutions to the Categorical Problem

In this section, we explore a number of ideas related to categorical data in SEM. The nontechnical reader will be relieved to know that we will conclude with some simpler techniques than the ensuing presentation would suggest.

One solution to this current dilemma is to conduct mediation analyses in which all three variables are treated similarly, all as continuous, or all as categorical, so that their differential measurement status doesn't lead to spurious evidence regarding the conclusions of the relative strengths of the direct and mediated paths. We have seen how to treat three continuous variables, namely, through SEM. If all three variables were categorical, log-linear models would be applicable. Logit models would seem to be appropriate because the mediation inquiry is a predictive one; that is, one in which a dependent variable is of interest (Menard, 1995). Yet there does not exist an easy translation of the SEM logic of modeling simultaneous equations (not even multiple structural equations, much less measurement equations) in the logit or log-linear modeling contexts. Let's see what the issues are.

For a binary dependent variable, Y, we would study the effect of predictors such as X and M by asking, "For an observation with any given combination of X and M values, how likely is it that Y takes on the value '1' versus '0' (the '1' usually signifying the presence of the behavior of interest)?" Specifically, given the particular values of X and M, what are the odds that $Y = 1$ versus $Y = 0$? Comparing those odds explicitly in a ratio format yields an "odds ratio," $[P(Y = 1)/(1 - P(Y = 1))]$. Multiplicative terms are always trickier than additive terms, so if we take the natural log, the so-called, logit:

$$\text{logit}(Y) = \ln(\text{odds}) = \ln\left[\frac{P(Y = 1)}{1 - P(Y = 1)}\right], \qquad [5.1]$$

then the model can be written as a function of the predictors in a familiar, linear format:

$$\text{logit}(Y) = \beta_0 + \beta_X X + \beta_M M. \qquad [5.2]$$

Fitting this logit model would yield fit statistics, and estimates of the parameters associated with the $X \rightarrow Y$ and $M \rightarrow Y$ paths.

The relationship between X and M is included implicitly (as it is, though not usually described as such, in Equation 2.3). As with the regression approach to mediation, a separate model, $\text{logit}(M) = \beta_0 + \beta_X X$, would have to be fit to explicitly tease out the $X \rightarrow M$ path. For example, Knoke and Burke (1980, p. 43) describe a multiple equation approach to fitting causal models with discrete data, and the model fitting is conducted in waves, for example, $X \rightarrow M$, then $M \rightarrow Y$ in our mediation application. Although both models are fit in the same statistical framework (i.e., logits), the results are not put together because the resulting "path coefficients" are not easily integrated and interpreted (as the $a \times b$ indirect path had been in SEM). Fienberg (1981) similarly illustrates an example in which blocks of precursor variables are entered into subsequent stages, building up to a prediction of the final endogenous variable. He is conservative regarding the interpretation of the "path coefficients," suggesting that rather than reporting estimates, researchers report only their signs.[7] Yet if we invert the logit equation from

$$\text{logit}(Y) = \ln\left[\frac{P(Y=1)}{1-P(Y=1)}\right] = \beta_X X + \beta_M M,$$

to solve for

$$P(Y=1) = \frac{e^{\beta_X X + \beta_M M}}{1 + e^{\beta_X X + \beta_M M}},$$

and assume that the $X \to M$ and $M \to Y$ paths were independent to enable taking the products of their respective probabilities (as in SEM when computing $a \times b$), and call that p_m (for the mediated probability), we could compare this probability with the probability that the data flow along the direct path, p_d, via a standard z test for proportions:

$$z = \frac{p_d - p_m}{\sqrt{\dfrac{p_d\left(1-p_d\right)}{n_d} + \dfrac{p_m\left(1-p_m\right)}{n_m}}}.$$

Still, while the categorical data causal model counterpart could be fit sequentially (like the old-fashioned regression approach), doing so would put us back in the scenario of fitting multiple models, a statistical action that we previously described as suboptimal.

Collins, Graham, and Flaherty (1998) take a different approach to mediation chains for binary data. They form a decision tree from X to M to Y, wherein the choices made at each point probabilistically determine one's endpoint—a conceptualization that seems especially well suited to binary mediation variables. If we think of mediation as a composition of the following links: $X \to M(\text{yes})$ or $X \to M(\text{no})$, then from each M node, $M(\text{yes}) \to Y(\text{yes})$ or $M(\text{yes}) \to Y(\text{no})$ and from $M(\text{no}) \to Y(\text{yes})$ or $M(\text{no}) \to Y(\text{no})$, we would have a decision tree starting from X branching first to M (yes or no), then branching again at Y (yes or no), creating four endpoint states:

1. $X \to M(\text{yes}) \to Y(\text{yes})$,

2. $X \to M(\text{yes}) \to Y(\text{no})$,

3. $X \to M(\text{no}) \to Y(\text{yes})$,

4. $X \to M(\text{no}) \to Y(\text{no})$.   [5.3]

A concern might be how to fit these four states, rather than just two in a binary logit. Yet the four states are not equally interesting. Consider that State 1 represents the mediation, indirect path. State 3 is the direct route from X to Y. State 2 is nothing of note (one path of the mediation is supported but the other is not). State 4 is similarly of no import (no direct or indirect support is obvious). Thus, while it first appeared that the four states would require more complex modeling, there are really only two states of interest—Condition 1 and Condition 3. These two states could easily be modeled in a logit, with States 2 and 4 effectively being dismissed (dropped as missing data). The resulting logit parameters then would express the "odds" that the path was indirect versus direct (a positive and significant β_X would indicate support for mediation, a negative and significant estimate would indicate support for the direct path, and partial mediation would be one way to interpret a nonsignificant parameter—unfortunately, lack of power is an omnipresent rival for nonsignificant findings).

Researchers interested in modeling all four states could run a multinomial logit; that is, a logit model for dependent variables with more than two categories. For example, imagine a dependent variable with three choices (easily extended to our four states): A, B, and C. The multinomial logit model uses a set of predictors, "x" to model pairs of categories. To simplify the conceptualization, pairs of adjacent categories are frequently modeled, and their transitivity is noted (cf. Long, 1997, p. 150):

$$\ln\left[\frac{P(A\mid x)}{P(B\mid x)}\right] + \ln\left[\frac{P(B\mid x)}{P(C\mid x)}\right] = \ln\left[\frac{P(A\mid x)}{P(C\mid x)}\right].$$

In our application, we could model states 1 through 4 as a function of X (M is contained in the creation of the four states).

For all this and other statistical machinery, the mediation question still ultimately reduces to a comparison of the strengths of a direct and indirect path. Winship and Mare (1983, pp. 83–84) take the equations of the SEM (Equation 3.20): $\hat{Y} = \Gamma X + BY + \Psi$, namely,

$$\begin{bmatrix} \hat{M} \\ \hat{Y} \end{bmatrix} = \begin{bmatrix} \gamma_{MX} \\ \gamma_{YX} \end{bmatrix} [X] + \begin{bmatrix} 0 & 0 \\ \beta_{YM} & 0 \end{bmatrix} \begin{bmatrix} M \\ Y \end{bmatrix} + \begin{bmatrix} \psi_M \\ \psi_Y \end{bmatrix} = \begin{bmatrix} \gamma_{MX} X + \psi_M \\ \gamma_{YX} X + \beta_{YM} M + \psi_Y \end{bmatrix}$$

and decompose the total effect of X on Y into the two central pieces, the direct effect of X on Y and the indirect effect of X on Y through M. For continuous Y, we know that would be $c + ab$, specifically in SEM notation, $\gamma_{YX} + (\gamma_{MX} \times \beta_{YM})$. Instead, if Y is discrete, Winship and Mare (pp. 83–84) start with the fundamentals:

$$\frac{dY}{dX} = \frac{\partial Y}{\partial X} + \frac{\partial Y}{\partial M}\frac{dM}{dX},$$

and plug in the logits, given the expected effects of X on the probability that $Y = 1$ (for a binary dependent variable):

$$\frac{dp(Y=1)}{dX} = \frac{\gamma_{YX}e(\gamma_{YX}X+\beta_{YM}M)}{[1+e(\gamma_{YX}X+\beta_{YM}M)]^2} + \frac{\beta_{YM}\gamma_{MX}e(\gamma_{YX}X+\beta_{YM}M)}{[1+e(\gamma_{YX}X+\beta_{YM}M)]^2}$$

$$= \gamma_{YX}p_Y(1-p_Y) + \beta_{YM}\gamma_{MX}p_Y(1-p_Y), \qquad [5.4]$$

where $p_y = p(Y = 1)$ (and is a little more complicated when Y is continuous but measured by a discrete indicator) and needs to be evaluated at each value of Y. However, since the $p_Y(1-p_Y)$ piece is in both parts of Equation 5.4, the focus of the investigation is still an examination of the comparative sizes of γ_{YX} and $\beta_{YM}\gamma_{MX}$.

So what is a researcher to make of all this? There may be a simple solution. Fitting a log-linear model among the three variables with all two-way effects would allow the examination of the estimates for the $X \rightarrow Y$ and $M \rightarrow Y$ paths (as did the logit, in Equation 5.2), as well as the $X \rightarrow M$ path. The model would look like

$$\ln(f_{xmy}) = \beta_0 + \beta_X + \beta_M + \beta_Y + \beta_{MX} + \beta_{YX} + \beta_{YM}. \qquad [5.5]$$

Fit statistics would be generated, and the β_{MX}, β_{YX}, and β_{YM} estimates obtained.[8]

For the categorical data in Table 5.1, the log-linear model produces the estimates in Table 5.2.[9] Independent chi-squares are additive, so an approximate test for the relative size of the mediation links over the size of the direct path would be

$$\left(X^2_{MX} + X^2_{YM}\right) - X^2_{YX} = \Delta X^2_{\text{due-to-mediation}} \sim \chi^2_1.$$

For these data, $\Delta X^2_{\text{due-to-mediation}} = (191.57 + 540.09) - 482.98 = 248.68$, which is significant, $p < .05$ ($\chi^2_{1;.05} = 3.841$), meaning partial mediation

TABLE 5.2
Log-Linear Parameter Estimates of Categorical
X, M, and Y of Table 5.1

Model Parameter	Estimate	X^2
β_{XM}	0.296	191.57
β_{XY}	0.471	482.98
β_{MY}	0.493	540.09

NOTE: Each χ^2 is significant, $p < .0001$.

is supported (some variance is direct, given that the $X \rightarrow Y$ link was significant).

Other techniques have also been explored in the literature. Perhaps the most encompassing framework was that offered by Muthén (1984) employing polychoric correlations (for ordered variables). His technique is a sensitive method to help determine the thresholds of the category levels, but it requires large sample sizes. In other developments, preliminary results suggest it might be effective to fit a log-linear model and invert the covariance matrix of the parameter estimates (Kupek, 2005) as input to the structural equations model.

These solutions have been offered for three discrete variables. The question that remains is the integration of variables X, M, and Y when they differ in form (one or more continuous, one or more discrete). Logistic regressions are an extension of logits, also intended for discrete dependent variables, but allowing for continuous or discrete predictors. Hence, logistic regressions could model discrete M or Y as a function of mixed predictors, but the integration across models is difficult even if both equations are logistic. Even worse, they are noncomparable if one endogenous variable was continuous (requiring a general linear model) and one discrete (requiring a logit or logistic regression), given that the paths would have been estimated by such different means, using different techniques that make different assumptions and estimate parameters on such different scales (i.e., linear vs. log-odds). Such scenarios could not even be fit via mixing models across multiple waves of equations, such as in hierarchically nested models, because outputs of linear (or logit) functions would serve as input into logit (or linear) functions.[10]

Recall that the primary concern with categorical variables is the inherent "loss of information." The loss has been demonstrated to lead to an underestimation of the size of factor loadings (for the categorical variables) and an overestimation of the chi-square values (DiStefano, 2002; Schumacker & Beyerlein, 2000). Note that both results err in the statistically conservative direction. Some simulation results suggest that results based on categorical variables approximated those of their continuous counterparts, except in the extreme case where dichotomous variables were skewed in opposite directions (Ethington, 1987).

For the researcher working with categorical data, here is the bottom line: If all variables are categorical, a log-linear model may be fit, per Equation 5.5. In general, if the variables X, M, and Y are any mix of categorical and continuous, SEM seems to be the primary solution (with the categorical variables represented as dummy variables), as demonstrated previously. SEM might result in some relationship truncation, but at least it is a conservative statistical approach. It allows for the mix of continuous and discrete variables (as would logistic regressions, but it further allows the comparison with other models, rather than needing to translate back and forth between SEM and logits).

5.4 Longitudinal Data

Occasionally, researchers have repeated measures, or within-subjects, data in which they wish to estimate mediation models. Some techniques have been offered to address these new concerns (cf. Cole & Maxwell, 2003; Judd, Kenny, & McClelland, 2001), but once again, repeated measures data may be incorporated easily into structural equations models.

Figure 5.4 shows the nature of the repeated measures data—measures of X, M, and Y are obtained at Times 1 and 2, and the researcher investigates the usual structural parameters; that is, estimating $X_1 \rightarrow M_1 \rightarrow Y_1$ and $X_1 \rightarrow Y_1$ and $X_2 \rightarrow M_2 \rightarrow Y_2$ and $X_2 \rightarrow Y_2$. The new twist is that the within-subjects nature of the data is handled through correlating the error structures. Specifically, one would allow the measurement error terms to be correlated for X_1 and X_2 (i.e., $\theta_{\delta(X_1,X_2)}$ is now estimated, not fixed at zero), and analogously for the measurement error terms for M_1 and M_2, and Y_1 and Y_2 (i.e., $\theta_{\varepsilon(M_1,M_2)}$ and $\theta_{\varepsilon(Y_1,Y_2)}$ are estimated, not fixed at zero). These correlated errors are estimated parameters (as are their variances in order to allow the covariance to vary and be estimated).

The LISREL syntax follows to fit a model such as that depicted in Figure 5.4.

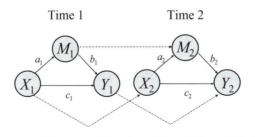

Figure 5.4 Mediation With Repeated Measures

Title: mediation among X,Y,Z at times 1&2, and correlated errors between like terms.
da ni=6 no=100 ma=cm
la
x1 m1 y1 x2 m2 y2
cm sy
1.00
0.30 1.00
0.30 0.30 1.00
0.30 0.30 0.30 1.00
0.30 0.30 0.30 0.30 1.00
0.30 0.30 0.30 0.30 0.30 1.00
se
m1 y1 m2 y2 x1 x2
mo ny=4 ne=4 nx=2 nk=2 lx=fu,fr td=fu,fr ly=fu,fr te=fu,fr be=fu,fr ga=fu,fr
pa ga
1 0
1 0
0 1
0 1
pa be
0 0 0 0
1 0 0 0
0 0 0 0
0 0 1 0
pa lx
0 0
0 0
pa td
1 1
1 1
pa ly
1 0 1 0
0 1 0 1
1 0 1 0
0 1 0 1
pa te
0 0 0 0
0 0 0 0
0 0 0 0
0 0 0 0
va 1.0 lx(1,1) lx(2,2) ly(1,1) ly(2,2) ly(3,3) ly(4,4)
out me=ml is sf

The parameter estimates that capture the correlations between measurement errors of identical constructs measured at multiple points in time may be of interest in and of themselves. For example, if they are all near zero, it might indicate that the sample respondents are making no efforts in being consistent over time, or it might suggest that the impact of the measurement experience at Time 1 on Time 2 was minor, and so on. Typically, these estimates are not of focal interest; rather, they are included in the model to purify the estimation of the structural path coefficients, which are of greater theoretical interest.

Regarding the structural coefficients, a researcher may compare the strength of the direct and indirect paths at both Times 1 and 2, via the z test in Equation 2.4. In addition, the equation may be used to quantify the comparison of the direct path at Time 1 to the direct path at Time 2, and similarly for the indirect paths. Researchers may then conclude that the extent of mediation has strengthened or weakened over time. If the z test comparing the paths over time is insignificant, it may be that the structure of mediation had not changed, or that the sample sizes were too small to detect the change.

Notes

1. Note that the model is not conceptualized as $X_1 \rightarrow X_1 *X_2$ and $X_2 \rightarrow X_1 *X_2$ (and then $X_1 *X_2 \rightarrow M$, etc.). While this structure has some intuitive appeal, given that X_1 and X_2 in a sense "contribute" to the product/interaction term, they did so already in the computation of the $X_1 *X_2$ term that is already included in the covariance matrix. They do not "cause" $X_1 *X_2$ in the SEM sense. Furthermore, in ANOVA or any general linear model, the three terms, the main effects X_1 and X_2, and the interaction term, $X_1 *X_2$, are estimable independently, and with balanced data they are orthogonal effects; hence, it would be misleading to model $X_1 \rightarrow X_1 *X_2$ and $X_2 \rightarrow X_1 *X_2$. The syntax models each of X_1, X_2, and $X_1 *X_2$ as separable exogenous variables, each of which has a path to M and another to Y. The paths extending from the main effects serve as statistical controls, and the paths extending from the interaction term are the ones of interest, in a mediated moderation model.

2. Cortina, Chen, and Dunlap (2001) offer an overview of the issues and Moulder and Algina (2002) offer a preliminary comparison among several alternative analytical approaches. There are concerns with multicollinearity among predictor terms, with suggestions such as residual- or mean-centering the main effect variables before creating the cross-product term (Little, Bovaird, & Widaman, 2006). There are also simple logistical problems, for example, in the presence of multiple indicators, the inclusion of interactive product terms would imply that products be computed between pairs of indicators of the main effect variables, generating many more terms, which is less parsimonious than a simpler computation based on

a single product of the factor scores (Algina & Moulder, 2001; Schumacker, 2002). Finally, Ping (1996a, 1996b, 1996c) suggests that better estimation is achieved if the measurement part of the model is conducted first, then the measurement estimates used as input constants to fit the structural coefficients.

3. Winship and Mare (1983) provide a nice discussion of the differences between measures of inherently discrete phenomena (for which we posit probability models, e.g., traditionally analyzing such data via log-linear and logit models, p. 60), and discrete variables that serve as indicators of underlying continuous variables (for which we typically implicitly posit threshold models, and such data are typically analyzed via psychometric and econometric approaches, p. 58). They also discuss the nonlinear, stochastic relationship between the two (pp. 61–62). Purists would argue that ratings scales, as typically collected and analyzed, are almost never truly continuous, for example, not just rating scales, scores of 1 through 7, but even measuring length in inches, or say, "measuring" attitudes via cursor clicks on continuous-appearing lines on a screen (Bollen, 1989, p. 433).

4. Results are similar for varying levels of mediation (e.g., more or less variance going directly from $X \to Y$ or indirectly through M). Results are also similar, though fuzzier, for smaller sample sizes.

5. Bollen (1989, p. 435) reports some of the research conducted on investigating the behavior of Pearson product-moment correlation coefficients for discrete variables. Such research consistently says correlations (or parameters based on correlations, such as factor loadings, which he mentions, but also presumably path coefficients) are attenuated (i.e., they will be underestimated), and their standard errors are usually overestimated. These results highlight the classic findings that are of some comfort in suggesting that at least the results are more conservative (not likely prone to Type I errors in hypothesis testing). The attenuation of the strength of the relationship seems to worsen as the number of categories is reduced (e.g., < 5). The particularly problematic scenario is that in which a correlation is computed between two categorical variables whose data exhibit skews in the opposite directions.

6. In measurement theory, for the situation in which a categorical variable represents an underlying continuous quality, scholars discuss the substitution and replacement of data-based correlations that show the attenuation, with a polyserial correlation (when one variable is ordinal and the other is continuous), a polychoric correlation (when both variables are ordinal), or a tetrachoric correlation (when both variables are binary). These indices effectively estimate the correlation as if on the underlying continuous variable (cf. Bollen, 1989, p. 442). This preprocessing treatment of the data can be done in LISREL (through its accompanying program, Prelis). While there exists measurement theoretical support for such corrections, journal reviewers tend to be critical, since, after all, the adjustments make the correlations appear bigger.

7. Specifically, Fienberg (1981) says, "We view the assignment of numerical values as problematic, and we would limit ourselves to an indication of sign for causal relationships." (p. 121).

8. Just as in regression, the prediction results are said to be conditioned on the predictor variables, the relationships among which are in essence fixed, implying their relationship ought not be interpreted so much as they simply statistically control for sample characteristics of the data. Yet the relationships between X and M are estimable, and so if we're willing to assume an approximation, we can use the X, M relationship as a part of the $X \to M$, $M \to Y$ mediation link.

9. The reported statistics are Wald X^2s, defined as $(\beta_{XM} / SE(\beta_{XM}))^2$. Likelihood ratio test statistics can be computed instead (e.g., by specifying "Type3" in SAS), for researchers concerned about small samples.

10. Work on generalized linear modeling is an attempt to create an umbrella approach to thinking about a number of different models, analogous to the superordinate relationship of "general linear model" to both ANOVA and regression. In generalized linear models, a researcher's choice of an error distribution (e.g., normal, log-normal), the nature of the linking function between the predictors and dependent variable (e.g., linear, log-linear), results in what had superficially appeared to be different techniques (e.g., regression, logit models). Still, these techniques do not allow for the simultaneous estimation of two equations such as our structural equations,

$$\begin{bmatrix} \hat{M} \\ \hat{Y} \end{bmatrix} = \begin{bmatrix} \gamma_{MX} X + \psi_M \\ \gamma_{YX} X + \beta_{YM} M + \psi_Y \end{bmatrix},$$

where a discrete M would require the log-linear link and log-normal error distribution, and a continuous Y would require the linear link and normal error distribution.

CHAPTER 6. CONCLUSIONS

A mediation analysis is not always necessary. Many explanatory processes may be inferred from their resultant outcomes. If mediations are to be conducted, a strong theoretical basis is necessary, given the ambiguities introduced regarding the relationship between correlational data and the goal of making conclusive, causal statements. If the theoretical base is strong enough, the researcher should be capable of arguing and empirically testing against alternative models, for example, those in which the roles of the variables are interchanged or those in which the causal direction is reversed.

If mediation tests are to proceed, follow the steps that are given in Table 6.1 and summarized briefly here. Fit one model via structural equations models, in which the direct and indirect paths are fit simultaneously so as to estimate each effect while partialling out the other. Some extent of mediation is indicated when *both* of the $X \rightarrow M$ and $M \rightarrow Y$ coefficients are significant. If either is not (and certainly if both are not significant), the analyst stops and concludes that there is no mediation.

If some mediation is present (i.e., both indirect paths are significant), the z test (Equation 2.4) will be significant if the size of the mediated path is greater than the direct path. If the z is significant and the direct path $X \rightarrow Y$ is not, then the mediation is complete. If both the z and the direct path $X \rightarrow Y$ are significant, then the mediation is "partial" (with a significantly larger portion of the variance in Y due to X being explained via the indirect rather than direct path). If the z is not significant but the direct path $X \rightarrow Y$ is, then the mediation is "partial" (with statistically comparable sizes for the indirect and direct paths), in the presence of a direct effect. If neither the z nor the direct path $X \rightarrow Y$ is significant, then the mediation is "partial" (with statistically comparable sizes for the indirect and direct paths), in the absence of a direct effect.[1]

Ideally, each construct should be measured with three or more indicator variables (Bagozzi & Baumgartner, 1994). And ideally, the mediation should be embedded in a more extensive nomological network that contained at least one more construct, as an antecedent of X or a consequence of X, M, or Y.

Note

1. The researcher could consider reporting the "proportion of mediation" (i.e., $(\hat{a} \times \hat{b} / (\hat{a} \times \hat{b}) + \hat{c}))$; however, MacKinnon et al. (2002) have presented results that indicate that this ratio is rather unstable, except for very large samples.

TABLE 6.1

Summary Steps for Testing for Mediation via Structural Equations Models

1. To test for mediation, fit one model via structural equations models, so the direct and indirect paths are fit simultaneously to estimate either effect while partialling out, or statistically controlling for, the other.
   a. "Some" mediation is indicated when both the $X \to M$ and $M \to Y$ coefficients are significant.
   b. If either one is not significant (or if both are not significant), there is no mediation, and the researcher should stop.

2. Compute the z to test explicitly the relative sizes of the indirect (mediated) versus direct paths. Conclusions hold as follows:
   a. If the z is significant and the direct path $X \to Y$ is not, then the mediation is complete.
   b. If both the z and the direct path $X \to Y$ are significant, then the mediation is "partial" (with a significantly larger portion of the variance in Y due to X being explained via the indirect than direct path).
   c. If the z is not significant but the direct path $X \to Y$ is (and recall that the indirect, mediated path $X \to M$, $M \to Y$ is significant, or we would have ceased the analysis already), then the mediation is "partial" (with statistically comparable sizes for the indirect and direct paths), in the presence of a direct effect.
   d. If neither the z nor the direct path $X \to Y$ is significant, then the mediation is "partial" (with statistically comparable sizes for the indirect and direct paths), in the absence of a direct effect.

3. The researcher can report the results:
   a. Show the estimates (parameter estimates and standard errors) of the a, b, and c path coefficients, and the z test of Equation 2.4.
   b. Report the estimate that the SEM package provides for the "indirect effect" along with that for either the "direct effect" or the "total effect."
   c. If the researcher would like to make categorical statements, he or she can conclude (according to his or her results) that there is "no," "partial," or "full" mediation.

4. Ideally, each construct should be measured with three or more indicator variables.

5. The central trivariate mediation should be a structural subset of a more extensive nomological network that contained at least one more construct, as an antecedent of X or a consequence of X, M, or Y.

6. The researcher should acknowledge the possibility of rival models, and test several, at least $Y \to M \to X$, and something such as $M \to X \to Y$. Ideally, these rivals would be fit with Q, to have diagnostic fit statistics. However, alternative models should be run even with only X, M, and Y, and the researcher should be able to argue against the different parameter estimates as being less meaningful than their preferred model.

APPENDIX

Commands for Fitting SEM Mediation Models
via SAS, EQS, and AMOS

SAS (http://support.sas.com/onlinedoc/913/docMainpage.jsp)

```
proc calis data=mine cov modification primat toteff ;
*basic mediation;
var x m y; ram
1 3 2 betamy,
1 3 1 gamxy,
1 2 1 gamxm,
2 1 1 phix,
2 2 2 psim,
2 3 3 psiy; run;
```

```
proc calis data=mine cov modification primat toteff ;
*mediation with measures: 3 x vars, 3 mediator measures, 2 y measures;
var x1 x2 x3 m1 m2 m3 y1 y2; ram
1 1 9 lambx1, 1 2 9 lambx2, 1 3 9 lambx3, 1 4 10 lambm1, 1 5 10 lambm2,
1 6 10 lambm3, 1 7 11 lamby1, 1 8 11 lamdy2, 2 1 1 tdx1, 2 2 2 tdx2, 2 3 3 tdx3,
2 4 4 tem1, 2 5 5 tem2, 2 6 6 tem3, 2 7 7 tey1, 2 8 8 tey2,
1 11 10 betamy,
1 11 9 gamxy,
1 10 9 gamxm,
2 9 9 phix,
2 10 10 psim,
2 11 11 psiy; run;
```

```
proc calis data=mine cov modification primat toteff ;
*4 vars, add q->x;
var x m y q; ram
1 3 2 betamy,
1 3 1 gamxy,
1 2 1 gamxm,
1 1 4 newlink,
2 1 1 phix, 2 4 4 phiq, 2 1 4 phixq,
2 2 2 psim,
2 3 3 psiy; run;
```

71

```
proc calis data=mine cov modification primat toteff ;
*longer chain, x->m1->m2->y;
var x m1 m2 y; ram
1 4 3 betam2y,  1 3 2 bm1m2,
1 4 1 gamxy,
1 2 1 gamxm1,
2 1 1 phix,
2 2 2 psim1, 2 3 3 psim2
2 4 4 psiy; run;

proc calis data=mine cov modification primat toteff ;
*add interaction term;
var x1 x2 x1x2 m y; ram
1 3 2 betamy,
1 4 1 gamx1m, 1 4 2 gamx2m, 1 4 3 gamintm,
1 5 1 gamx1y, 1 5 2 gamx2y, 1 5 3 gaminty,
2 1 1 phix,
2 2 2 psim,
2 3 3 psiy; run;

proc calis data=mine cov modification primat toteff ;
*longitudinal, allow autocorrelations;
var x1 m1 y1 x2 m2 y2; ram
1 3 2 betamy1, 1 6 5 betamy2,
1 2 1 gamxm1, 1 5 4 gamxm2,
1 3 1 gamxy1, 1 6 4 gamxy2,
2 1 4 timex, 2 2 5 timem, 2 3 6 timey,
2 1 1 phix,
2 2 2 psim1,
2 3 3 psiy1, 2 4 4 psix2, 2 5 5 psim2, 2 6 6 psiy2; run;
```

EQS (http://www.mvsoft.com/products.htm)

```
/TITLE
My Mediation with Three Constructs, One Measure Each.
/SPECIFICATIONS
CASE=100; VAR=3; ME=ML; MA=COV;
/MATRIX
```

```
1.00
0.30 1.00
0.30 0.30 1.00
/LABELS
V1=X; V2=M; V3=Y;
F1=X; F2=M; F3=Y;
/EQUATIONS
F2 = *F1 + D2;
F3 = *F1 + *F2 + D3;
/VARIANCES
D2 = *; D3 = *; F1 = *;
/END
```

```
/TITLE
Mediation adding the measurement model, with 3Xs, 3Ms, 2Ys.
/SPECIFICATIONS
CASE=100; VAR=8; ME=ML; MA=COV;
/MATRIX
1.00
0.30 1.00
0.30 0.30 1.00
0.30 0.30 0.30 1.00
0.30 0.30 0.30 0.30 1.00
0.30 0.30 0.30 0.30 0.30 1.00
0.30 0.30 0.30 0.30 0.30 0.30 1.00
0.30 0.30 0.30 0.30 0.30 0.30 0.30 1.00
/LABELS
V1=X1; V2=X2; V3=X3; V4=M1; V5=M2; V6=M3; V7=Y1; V8=Y2;
/EQUATIONS
F2 = *F1 + D2;
F3 = *F1 + *F2 + D3;
X1= *F1 +E1; X2= *F1 +E2; X3= *F1 +E3;
M1= *F2 +E4; M2= *F2 +E5; M3= *F2 +E6;
Y1= *F3 +E7; Y2= *F3 +E8;
/VARIANCES
D2 = *; D3 = *; F1 = *; E1=*; E2=*; E3=*; E4=*; E5=*; E6=*; E7=*; E8=*;
/END
```

```
/TITLE
Four constructs, add q->x.
/SPECIFICATIONS
```

```
CASE=100; VAR=4; ME=ML; MA=COV;
/MATRIX
1.00
0.30 1.00
0.30 0.30 1.00
0.30 0.30 0.30 1.00
/LABELS
V1=X; V2=M; V3=Y; V4=Q;
F1=X; F2=M; F3=Y; F4=Q ;
/EQUATIONS
F1= *F4 + D4 ;
F2 = *F1 + D2;
F3 = *F1 + *F2 + D3;
/VARIANCES
D2 = *; D3 = *; D4=*; F1 = *;
/END

/TITLE
Longer chain, X->M1->M2->Y.
/SPECIFICATIONS
CASE=100; VAR=4; ME=ML; MA=COV;
/MATRIX
1.00
0.30 1.00
0.30 0.30 1.00
0.30 0.30 0.30 1.00
/LABELS
V1=X; V2=M1; V3=M2; V4=Y;
F1=X; F2=M1; F3=M2; F4=Y;
/EQUATIONS
F2 = *F1 + D2;
F3 = *F2 + D4;
F4 = *F1 + *F3 + D3;
/VARIANCES
D2 = *; D3 = *; D4=*; F1 = *;
/END

/TITLE
Add interaction term.
/SPECIFICATIONS
CASE=100; VAR=5; ME=ML; MA=COV;
/MATRIX
1.00
```

```
0.30 1.00
0.30 0.30 1.00
0.30 0.30 0.30 1.00
0.30 0.30 0.30 0.30 1.00
/LABELS
V1=X1; V2=X2; V3=X1X2; V4=M; V5=Y;
F1=X1; F2=X2; F3=X1X2; F4=M; F5=Y;
/EQUATIONS
F4 = *F1 + *F2 + *F3 + D2;
F5 = *F1 + *F2 + *F3 + *F4 + D3;
/VARIANCES
D2 = *; D3 = *; F1 = *; F2 = *;
/END

/TITLE
Longitudinal, as in Figure 5.4.
/SPECIFICATIONS
CASE=100; VAR=6; ME=ML; MA=COV;
/MATRIX
1.00
0.30 1.00
0.30 0.30 1.00
0.30 0.30 0.30 1.00
0.30 0.30 0.30 0.30 1.00
0.30 0.30 0.30 0.30 0.30 1.00
/LABELS
V1=X1; V2=M1; V3=Y1; V4=X2; V5=M2; V6=Y2;
F1=X1; F2=M1; F3=Y1; F4=X2 ; F5=M2 ; F6=Y2 ;
/EQUATIONS
F2 = *F1 + D2;
F3 = *F1 + *F2 + D3;
F5 = *F4 + *F2 + D4;
F6 = *F4 + *F5 + *F3 + D5;
F4 = *F1 + D6;
/VARIANCES
D2 = *; D3 = *; D4 = *; D5 = *; F1 = *;
/END
```

AMOS (spss.com/amos)

For most users, the pleasure of working with the AMOS software is that it offers a graphical interface. Hence, to write out commands rather defeats the purpose. Nevertheless, the syntax is offered below for the basic mediation:

```
Sub Main
  Dim Sem as New AmosEngine
  'Input File for My Mediation'
  SEM.BeginGroup "C:Myfile.nam"
  Sem.Structure "Y←M"
  Sem.Structure "Y←X"
  Sem.Structure "M←X"
End Sub
```

For the remaining modeling alternatives presented in the book, after the data are imported, drawing tools are available for drawing constructs and variables, and arrows for links between them.

- To emulate the measurement model incorporated into the mediation analysis, the AMOS drawing (before hitting "run") should resemble Figure 3.1 (albeit with 3 Xs, 3 Ms, and 2 Ys).

- To mimic the model with four constructs, in which Q is an antecedent to X, the AMOS figure should resemble Figure 4.2a.

- For a longer chain, such as $X \rightarrow M_1 \rightarrow M_2 \rightarrow Y$, in addition to these arrows, there should also be included the direct link from $X \rightarrow Y$.

- To include a moderator, five variables would be represented: X_1, X_2, X_1X_2 (the product), M, Y, with all links from X_1, X_2, X_1X_2 to both M and Y, and a final link from $M \rightarrow Y$.

- Finally, for the longitudinal mediation depicted in Figure 5.4, there would be links: $X_1 \rightarrow M_1$, $X_1 \rightarrow Y_1$, $M_1 \rightarrow Y_1$, and $X_2 \rightarrow M_2$, $X_2 \rightarrow Y_2$, $M_2 \rightarrow Y_2$. In addition, the user must provide for the autocorrelation links, that is, links from $X_1 \rightarrow X_2$, $M_1 \rightarrow M_2$, $Y_1 \rightarrow Y_2$.

MPlus (http://www.statmodel.com/index.shtml)

```
TITLE:      initial three variable mediation
DATA:       FILE IS my1.dat;
VARIABLE:   NAMES ARE x m y;
MODEL:      y ON x m;
            m ON x;
```

TITLE: mediation with 3 Xs, 3 Ms, 2 Ys
DATA: FILE IS my2.dat;
VARIABLE: NAMES ARE x1-x3 m1-m3 y1 y2;
MODEL: f1 BY x1-x3;
     f2 BY m1-m3;
     f3 BY y1-y2;
     y ON x m;
     m ON x;

TITLE: adding q as fourth construct
DATA: FILE IS my3.dat;
VARIABLE: NAMES ARE x m y q;
MODEL: y ON x m;
     m ON x;
     x ON q;

TITLE: longer chain, x to m1 to m2 to y
DATA: FILE IS my4.dat;
VARIABLE: NAMES ARE x m1 m2 y;
MODEL: y ON x m2;
     m2 ON m1;
     m1 ON x;

TITLE: including a moderator
DATA: FILE IS my5.dat;
VARIABLE: NAMES ARE x1 x2 x1x2 m y;
MODEL: y ON x1 x2 x1x2 m;
     m ON x1 x2 x1x2;

TITLE: longitudinal
DATA: FILE IS my6.dat;
VARIABLE: NAMES ARE x1 m1 y1 x2 m2 y2;
MODEL: y1 ON x1 m1;
     m1 ON x1;
     y2 ON x2 m2 y1;
     m2 ON x2 m1;
     x2 ON x1;

REFERENCES

Algina, J., & Moulder, B. C. (2001). A note on estimating the Joreskog-Yang model for latent variable interaction using LISREL 8.3. *Structural Equation Modeling, 8*(1), 40–52.

Asher, H. B. (1983). *Causal models* (2nd ed.). Beverly Hills, CA: Sage.

Bagozzi, R. P., & Baumgartner, H. (1994). The evaluation of structural equation models and hypothesis testing. In R. P. Bagozzi (Ed.), *Principles of marketing research* (pp. 386–422). Cambridge, MA: Blackwell.

Baron, R. M., Kenny, D. A. (1986). The moderator mediator variable distinction in social psychological research: Conceptual, strategic, and statistical considerations. *Journal of Personality and Social Psychology, 51*(6), 1173–1182.

Baumrind, D. (1983). Specious causal attributions in the social sciences. *Journal of Personality and Social Psychology, 45*(6), 1289–1298.

Bentler, P. (2001). Mediation. *Journal of Consumer Psychology, 10*(1/2), 84.

Bollen, K. A. (1987). Total, direct, and indirect effects in structural equation models. *Sociological Methodology, 17,* 37–69.

Bollen, K. A. (1989). Structural equations with latent variables. New York: Wiley.

Breckler, S. J. (1990). Applications of covariance structure modeling in psychology: Cause for concern? *Psychological Bulletin, 107*(2), 260–273.

Brown, R. L. (1997). Assessing specific mediational effects in complex theoretical models. *Structural Equation Modeling, 4*(2), 142–156.

Churchill, G. A., Jr., & Iacobucci, D. (2005). *Marketing research: Methodological foundations* (9th ed.). Mason, OH: Thomson Learning.

Cole, D. A., & Maxwell, S. E. (2003). Testing mediational models with longitudinal data: Questions and tips in the use of structural equation modeling. *Journal of Abnormal Psychology, 112*(4), 558–577.

Collins, L. M., Graham, J. W., & Flaherty, B. P. (1998). An alternative framework for defining mediation. *Multivariate Behavioral Research, 33*(2), 295–312.

Cortina, J. M., Chen, G., & Dunlap, W. P. (2001). Testing interaction effects in LISREL: Examination and illustration of available procedures. *Organizational Research Methods, 4*(4), 324–360.

Cote, J. (2001). Mediation. *Journal of Consumer Psychology, 10*(1/2), 93–94.

Cronbach, L., & Meehl, P. (1955). Construct validity in psychological tests. *Psychological Bulletin, 52*(4), 281–302.

Davis, J. A. (1985). *The logic of causal order.* Beverly Hills, CA: Sage.

DiStefano, C. (2002). The impact of categorization with confirmatory factor analysis. *Structural Equation Modeling, 9*(3), 327–346.

Ethington, C. A. (1987). The robustness of LISREL estimates in structural equation models with categorical variables. *Journal of Experimental Education, 55*(2), 80–88.

Fienberg, S. E. (1981). *The analysis of cross-classified categorical data* (2nd ed.). Cambridge: MIT Press.

Glymour, C. (2001). *The mind's arrows: Bayes nets and graphical causal models in psychology.* Cambridge: MIT Press.

Goodman, L. (1960). On the exact variance of products. *Journal of the American Statistical Association, 55,* 708–713.

Haughton, D., Kamis, A., & Scholten, P. (2006). A review of three directed acyclic graphs software packages: MIM, Tetrad, and WinMine. *The American Statistician, 60*(3), 272–286.

80

Hayduk, L., Cummings, G., Stratkotter, R., Nimmo, M., Grygoryev, K., Dosman, D., et al. (2003). Pearl's D-Separation: One more step into causal thinking. *Structural Equation Modeling, 10*(2), 289–311.

Holbert, R. L., & Stephenson, M. T. (2003). The importance of indirect effects in media effects research: Testing for mediation in structural equation modeling. *Journal of Broadcasting & Electronic Media, December,* 556–572.

Holland, P. W. (1986). Statistics and causal inference. *Journal of the American Statistical Association, 81*(396), 945–960.

Holland, P. W. (1988). Causal inference, path analysis, and recursive structural equations models. In C. C. Clogg (Ed.), *Sociological methodology* (Vol. 18, pp. 449–484). Washington, DC: American Sociological Association.

Humphreys, P., & Freedman, D. (1996). The grand leap. *British Journal of the Philosophy of Science, 47,* 113–123.

Iacobucci, D. (Ed.). (2001). Special issue on the methodological questions of the experimental behavioral researcher. *Journal of Consumer Psychology, 10*(1/2), 83–100.

Iacobucci, D., Saldanha, N., & Deng, J. X. (2007). A meditation on mediation: Evidence that structural equations models perform better than regressions. *Journal of Consumer Psychology, 17*(2), 140–154.

James, L. R., & Brett, J. M. (1984). Mediators, moderators, and tests for mediation. *Journal of Applied Psychology, 69*(2), 307–321.

James, L. R., Mulaik, S. A., & Brett, J. M. (1982). *Causal analysis: Assumptions, models, and data.* Beverly Hills, CA: Sage.

James, L. R., Mulaik, S. A., & Brett, J. M. (2007). A tale of two methods. Manuscript under review.

Jöreskog, K, & Sörbom, D. (1997). *LISREL 8: User's Reference Guide.* Chicago: SSI Scientific Software.

Judd, C. M., Kenny, D. A., & McClelland, G. H. (2001). Estimating and testing mediation and moderation in within-subject designs. *Psychological Methods, 6*(2), 115–134.

Karson, E. J., & Fisher, R. J. (2005). Reexamining and extending the dual mediation hypothesis in an on-line advertising context. *Psychology & Marketing, 22*(4), 333–351.

Kenny, D. A., Kashy, D. A., & Bolger, N. (1998). Data analysis in social psychology. In D. Gilbert, S. T. Fiske, & G. Lindzey (Eds.), *Handbook of social psychology* (Vol. 1, pp. 233–265). New York: McGraw-Hill.

Kline, R. B. (1998). Principles and practice of structural equation modeling. New York: Guilford Press.

Knoke, D., & Burke, P. J. (1980). *Log-linear models.* Beverly Hills, CA: Sage.

Kupek, E. (2005). Log-linear transformation of binary variables: A suitable input for SEM. *Structural Equation Modeling, 12*(1), 28–40.

Lee, S., & Hershberger, S. (1990). A simple rule for generating equivalent models in covariance structure modeling. *Multivariate Behavioral Research, 25*(3), 313–334.

Lehmann, D. (2001). Mediation. *Journal of Consumer Psychology, 10*(1/2), 90–92.

Little, T. D., Bovaird, J. A., & Widaman, K. A. (2006). On the merits of orthogonalizing powered and product terms: Implications for modeling interactions among latent variables. *Structural Equation Modeling, 13*(4), 497–519.

Long, J. S. (1997). Regression models for categorical and limited dependent variables. Thousand Oaks, CA: Sage.

Long, J. S. (2006). Covariance structure models: An introduction to LISREL. Thousand Oaks, CA: Sage.

Lynn, H. S. (2003). Suppression and confounding in action. *The American Statistician, 57*(1), 58–61.

MacCallum, R. C., Wegener, D. T., Uchino, B. N., & Fabrigar, L. R. (1993). The problem of equivalent models in applications of covariance structure analysis. *Psychological Bulletin, 114*(1), 185–199.

Mackie, J. L. (1974, 1980). *The cement of the universe: A study of causation.* Oxford, UK: Clarendon Press.

MacKinnon, D. P., Krull, J. L., & Lockwood, C. M. (2000). Equivalence of the mediation, confounding and suppression effect. *Prevention Science, 1*(4), 173–181.

MacKinnon, D. P., Lockwood, C. M., Hoffman, J. M., West, S. G., & Sheets, V. (2002). A comparison of methods to test mediation and other intervening variable effects. *Psychological Methods, 7*(1), 83–104.

MacKinnon, D. P., Lockwood, C. M., & Williams, J. (2004). Confidence limits for the indirect effect: Distribution of the product and resampling methods. *Multivariate Behavioral Research, 39*(1), 99–128.

MacKinnon, D. P., Warsi, G., & Dwyer, J. H. (1995). A simulation study of mediated effect measures. *Multivariate Behavioral Research, 30*(1), 41–62.

Mattanah, J. F., Hancock, G. R., & Brand, B. L. (2004). Parental attachment, separation-individuation, and college student adjustment: A structural equation analysis of mediational effects. *Journal of Counseling Psychology, 51*(2), 213–225.

McDonald, R. (2001). Mediation. *Journal of Consumer Psychology, 10*(1/2), 92–93.

McDonald, R. (2002). What can we learn from the path equations? Identifiability, constraints, equivalence. *Psychometrika, 67*(2), 225–249.

McKim, V. R., & Turner, S. P. (1997). *Causality in crisis? Statistical methods and the search for causal knowledge in the social sciences.* South Bend, IN: Notre Dame Press.

Menard, S. (1995). *Applied logistic regression analysis.* Thousand Oaks, CA: Sage.

Mill, J. S. (2002). *A system of logic: Ratiocinative and inductive.* Honolulu, HI: University Press of the Pacific.

Moulder, B. C., & Algina, J. (2002). Comparison of methods for estimating and testing latent variable interactions. *Structural Equation Modeling, 9*(1), 1–19.

Muller, D., Judd, C. M., & Yzerbyt, V. Y. (2005). When moderation is mediated and mediation is moderated. *Journal of Personality and Social Psychology, 89*(6), 852–863.

Muthén, B. (1984). A general structural equation model with dichotomous, ordered categorical, and continuous latent variable indicators. *Psychometrika, 49*(1), 115–132.

Netemeyer, R. (2001). Mediation. *Journal of Consumer Psychology, 10*(1/2), 83–84.

Pearl, J. (2000). *Causality: Models, reasoning, and inference.* Cambridge, UK: Cambridge University Press.

Pearl, J. (2001). Direct and indirect effects. *Proceedings of the 17th conference on Uncertainty in Artificial Intelligence* (pp. 411–420). San Francisco: Morgan Kaufmann.

Ping, R. A., Jr. (1996a). Estimating latent variable interactions and quadratics: The state of this art. *Journal of Management, 22*(1), 163–183.

Ping, R. A., Jr. (1996b). Latent variance interaction and quadratic effect estimation: A two-step technique using structural equation analysis. *Psychological Bulletin, 119*(1), 166–175.

Ping, R. A., Jr. (1996c). Latent variance regression: A technique for estimating interaction and quadratic coefficients. *Multivariate Behavioral Research, 31*(1), 95–120.

Preacher, K. J., & Hayes, A. F. (2004). SPSS and SAS procedures for estimating indirect effects in simple mediation models. *Behavior Research Methods, Instruments, & Computers, 36*(4), 717–731.

Preacher, K. J., & Hayes, A. F. (2006). Asymptotic and resampling strategies for assessing and comparing indirect effects in simple and multiple mediator models. Unpublished manuscript.

Rubin, D. B. (1974). Estimating causal effects of treatments in randomized and nonrandomized studies. *Journal of Educational Psychology, 66*(5), 688–701.

Rubin, D. B. (2005). Causal inference using potential outcomes: Design, modeling, decisions. *Journal of the American Statistical Association, 100*(469), 322–331.

Salmon, W. C. (1997). *Causality and explanation.* Oxford, UK: Oxford University Press.

Schumacker, R. E. (2002). Latent variable interaction modeling. *Structural Equation Modeling, 9*(1), 40–54.

Schumacker, R. E., & Beyerlein, S. T. (2000). Confirmatory factor analysis with different correlation types and estimation methods. *Structural Equation Modeling, 7*(4), 629–636.

Shadish, W. R. (1996). Meta-analysis and the exploration of causal mediating processes: A primer of examples, methods, and issues. *Psychological Methods, 1*(1), 47–65.

Shafer, G. (1996). *The art of causal conjecture.* Boston: MIT Press.

Shipley, B. (2000). A new inferential test for path models based on directed acyclic graphs. *Structural Equation Modeling, 7*(2), 206–218.

Shrout, P. E., & Bolger, N. (2002). Mediation in experimental and nonexperimental studies: New procedures and recommendations. *Psychological Methods, 7*(4), 422–445.

Simon, H. (1957). Spurious correlations: A causal interpretation. In *Models of man: Social and rational* (pp. 37–49). New York: Wiley.

Sobel, M. E. (1982). Asymptotic confidence intervals for indirect effects in structural equation models. In S. Leinhardt (Ed.), *Sociological methodology* (pp. 290–312). San Francisco: Jossey-Bass.

Sosa, E., & Tooley, M. (Eds.). (1993). *Causation.* Oxford, UK: Oxford University Press.

Spencer, S. J., Zanna, M. P., & Fong, G. T. (2005). Establishing a causal chain: Why experiments are often more effective than mediational analyses in examining psychological processes. *Journal of Personality and Social Psychology, 89*(6), 845–851.

Spirtes, P., Glymour, C., & Scheines, R. (2001). *Causation, prediction, and search: Adaptive computation and machine learning* (2nd ed.). New York: Bradford Books.

Suppes, P. (1970). *A probabilistic theory of causality.* Amsterdam: North-Holland.

Stelzl, I. (1986). Changing a causal hypothesis without changing the fit: Some rules for generating equivalent path models. *Multivariate Behavioral Research, 21,* 309–331.

Tzelgov, J., & Henik, A. (1991). Suppression situations in psychological research: Definitions, implications, and applications. *Psychological Bulletin, 109*(3), 524–536.

Winship, C., & Mare, R. D. (1983). Structural equations and path analysis for discrete data. *American Journal of Sociology, 89*(1), 54–110.

INDEX